Time, Space, and Material

Anne-Catrin Schultz

Time, Space, and Material

The Mechanics of Layering in Architecture

Edition Axel Menges

Expressing my gratitude to Stanford Anderson, Robert Clocker, Dorothea Duwe, John Habraken, Axel Menges, Guido Pietropoli, Hans-Joachim Schultz and the rest of my family as well as my colleagues in different parts of the world who have encouraged and assisted this project.

ISBN 978-3-936681-88-8

Printing and binding: Graspo CZ, a.s., Zlín, Czech Republic

Editing: Marilyn Novell
Graphics for layering diagrams: John Breda
Design: Axel Menges
Layout: Helga Danz

Contents

»Long before the human spirit was moved to build, a movement to create structure existed in the universe, and thus layers and joints were formed. And so it has remained to this day. Just as we erect our walls, the earth, since the beginning of time, has been creating layer by layer from the precipitation of the air and the sediments of the water.« Rudolf Schwarz[1]

1. Archaeological site exposing layers of the city, Verona, Italy.

Introduction

Urban areas and architecture can be seen as the product of continuous change – change that in many instances accumulates as layers of sediment. Our cities and buildings are continuously exposed to additions and subtractions according to changes in the built environment but also according to changes in social structures, use patterns, technology, transportation, and economy. Archaeologists uncover layers of different cities and settlements constructed on top of each other over centuries, seemingly never reaching a final state. City fabrics are a puzzle composed of building blocks, grids, and development patterns based on a variety of urban planning strategies to be used by different people. Over time, generations of vehicles and transportation systems, information technology, and communication are embedded, connecting the physical world with the virtual world. Buildings themselves are created from a series of layers defining the skins that separate outside from inside. Cultural and interpretative layers complement the physical world, adding immaterial strata to all of it.

This book explores the term layering and its application in the built environment. It provides examples of scholarly writing that address »layering« and present a theoretical framework for a widely used architectural idiom. These observations, in an attempt to put a face on a term that is commonly used but only rarely defined, reside in the spheres of narration, analysis, and speculation. The consideration of such a broad term will undoubtedly lead to omissions and certainly allow diverging opinions regarding how to define layering as a principle of architectural design and composition.

Layered systems are all around us, literally and phenomenally, possibly identifiable as the simultaneous existence of matter and content that usually does not necessitate, but often reflects, a hierarchy. As Rudolf Schwarz states in the opening quote, the physical conditions of our geological and man-made environment have been complemented by a system of computer-based operations and virtual spaces in which humans live in the 21st century. We continuously interact with layers of information provided by a multitude of sources and networks. In the realm of graphic design, many of us manage and evaluate different layers of data and information on a daily basis and have no problem identifying what we need to process. In architecture, buildings have been traditionally represented as ink drawings on sheets of vellum that could be laid on top of each other. Architectural CAD drawings and digital representations frequently are structured by systems of layers pertaining to topic areas within the project, to be turned on and off as needed, creating the same possibility of layering of information.

Edward R. Tufte writes about the layering of information that requires good planning and intelligent organization, especially when using computers; he anticipated that »all sorts of unplanned and lushly cluttered interacting combinations [will] turn up, with changing layers of information in miscellaneous windows surrounded by a frame of system commands and other computer administrative debris«.[2] Although at the time he wrote the book *Envisioning Information*, Tufte could not have anticipated the changes in information presentation that would come with the evolution of the worldwide web, he is quite clear about the need for proper relationships in graphic representation and two-dimensional layering. Moreover, he writes that the »layering of data, often achieved by felicitous subtraction of weight, enhances representation of both data dimensionality and density on flatland«.[3]

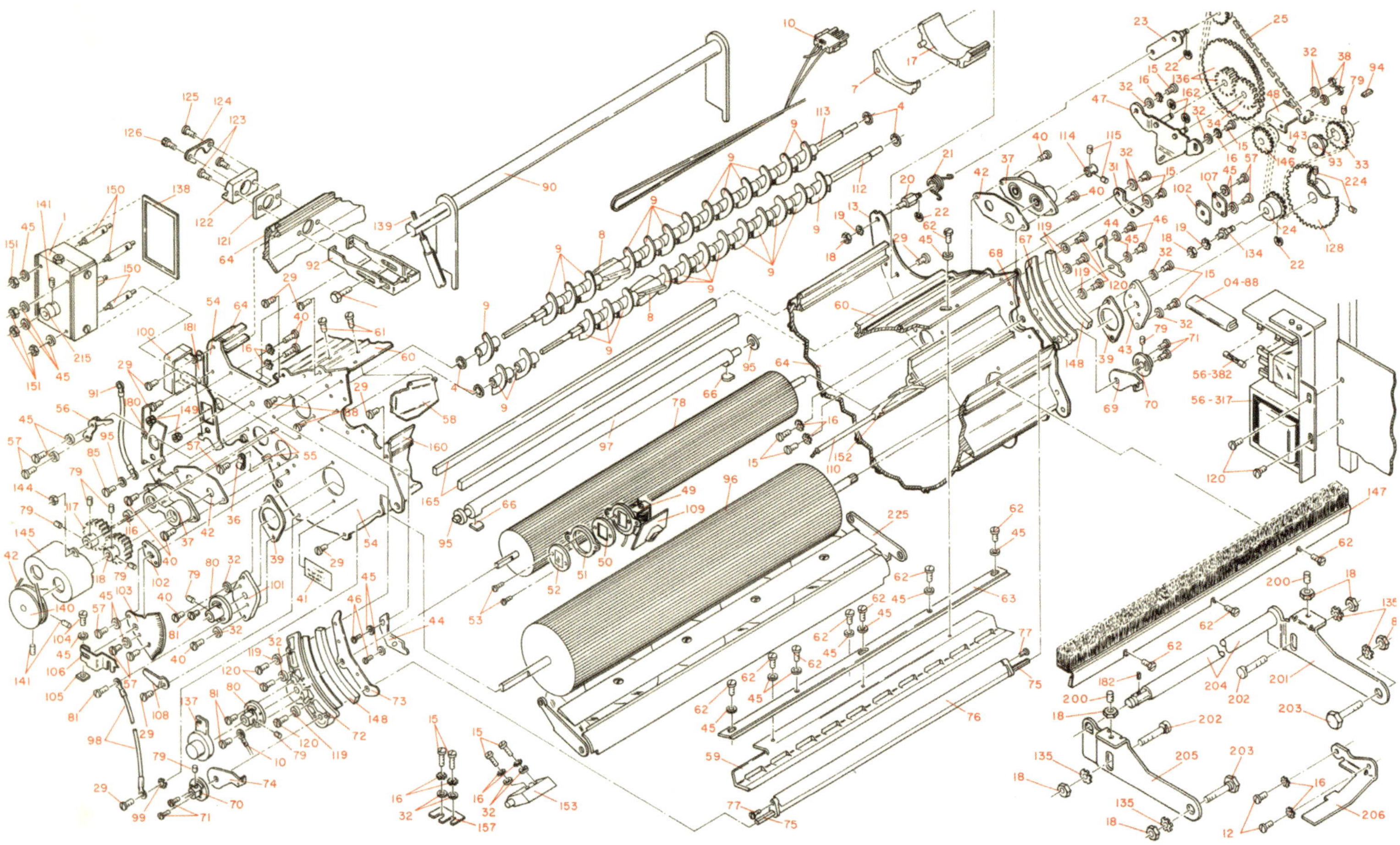

	am ◐																								
New York, NY	12.10	12.40	1.30	3.52	4.50	6.10	6.25	6.35	6.50	7.10	7.30	7.33	7.45	7.50	8.05	8.25	8.40	8.50	9.10	9.40	10.10	10.25	10.40	11.10	11.
Newark, NJP	12.24	12.55	1.44	4.07	5.04	6.24	6.38	6.49	7.04	7.24	7.45	7.47	7.59	8.04	8.19	8.39	8.54	9.04	9.24	9.54	10.24	10.39	10.54	11.24	11.
North Elizabeth										7.30	. .	. .	. .	8.10	. .	. .	. .	. .	. .	. .	. .	. .	. .	. .	.
Elizabeth	12.31	1.03	1.51	. .	5.11	6.31	. .	6.56	7.11	7.32	. .	7.54	. .	8.13	8.26	8.46	9.01	9.11	9.31	10.01	10.31	10.46	11.01	11.31	12.
Linden	12.36	. .	1.56	. .	5.16	6.36	. .	7.01	7.15	7.37	. .	7.59	. .	8.18	8.31	8.51	9.06	. .	9.36	10.06	10.36	. .	11.06	11.36	12.
North Rahway								7.03	. .	7.39	. .	. .	. .	8.20	8.33	8.54	. .	. .	. .	. .	. .	. .	. .	. .	.
Rahway	12.40	1.11	2.00	. .	5.20	6.40	. .	7.06	7.20	7.42	. .	8.03	. .	8.24	8.36	8.57	9.10	9.18	9.40	10.10	10.40	10.53	11.10	11.40	12.
Metro Park (Iselin)	12.44		2.04	4.26	5.24		6.56	7.10	7.25		8.04	8.07	8.15		8.40		9.14		9.44	10.14	10.44		11.14	11.44	12.
Metuchen	12.48		2.08	. .	5.28		. .	7.14	7.29		. .	8.11	. .		8.44		9.18		9.48	10.18	10.48		11.18	11.48	12.
Edison	12.51		2.11	. .	. .		. .	7.17	7.32		. .	8.14	. .		8.47		9.21		. .	10.21	. .		11.21	. .	12.
New Brunswick	12.55		2.15	. .	5.35		7.05	7.21	7.35		. .	8.18	8.25		8.50		9.25		9.54	10.25	10.54		11.25	11.54	12.
Jersey Avenue	1.02		2.18	. .	. .		. .	7.28	. .		. .	8.21	. .		. .		9.28		. .	10.28	. .		11.28	. .	12.
Princeton JunctionS			2.31	. .	5.50		7.19		7.50		. .	8.34	8.41		9.05		9.41		10.09	10.41	11.09		11.41	**12.09**	12.
Trenton, NJ			2.42	4.58	6.03		7.28		8.01		8.31	8.44	8.52		9.16		9.52		10.19	10.52	11.19		11.52	**12.19**	12.
TRAIN NUMBER	3701	3301	3801	67	3803	3201	51	3703	3807	3203	61	3809	47	3901	3811	3903	3813	3205	3815	3817	3819	3207	3821	3823	38
NOTES		XM		➤	3	3	➤ 3	3	3	3	➤ 3	3	➤ 3	3	3	3	3								

2. Edward Tufte, IBM Series III copier/duplicator, adjustment parts manual.
3. Edward Tufte, New Jersey Transit, northeastern corridor timetable.
4. Geological layering. Cross section through the Alps.

The meaning of layering

Although the term is broad by nature, its application in other fields is often more specific than in architecture. In architecture, layering can be the configuration of multiple surfaces, but is also associated with the notion of the skin of an object or building. A look at other disciplines reveals that the term »layering« is frequently used to refer to the simultaneous existence of planar elements or phenomena.

In the realm of engineering, layering is used to describe the analysis of materials and expresses the combination of materials in a single engineered product. The coating of materials is common practice – veneers have taken the place of formerly solid materials, causing purists to look for homogeneous materials rather than accepting the reduction of a material to millimeters.[4] In the political sciences, the term stratification refers to the »vertical structuring of the members of a society on the basis of socially relevant characteristics that influence the behavior of people toward each other«.[5]

In geology, layering refers to the deposits of various matter sedimented over time and altered by the earth's tectonic movements: »The type of stratification establishes the relative age of the rock strata.«[6] The order and composition of the layered assembly that is part of the Earth's crust contains information about the development of the geological formation. The chronological component of the succession is an essential component of the definition. In archaeology, too, the positions of individual strata contain information about how the strata align chronologically. The study of archaeology involves the analysis of how largely horizontal strata created as cultures, peoples, or settlements have declined and how they have been reorganized.

In the field of psychology, various theories are concerned with the stratification of the human personality and its repercussions. According to psychologist Wolfgang Viktor Ruttkowski, the development of each layer of personality is built on the layer that underlies it.[7] In a slightly different interpretation, the computer sciences articulate a layered architecture as an arrangement in which system components or network components are isolated in different layers in order to allow changes to be executed on one layer without impacting other layers of hardware or hardware.

A graphic design manual provides the following definition of the term related to information architecture: »Layering involves organizing information into related groupings and then presenting or making available only certain groupings at any one time. Layering is primarily used to manage complexity, but also can be used to reinforce relationships in information. […] Use two-dimensional layering to manage complexity and direct navigation through information. Consider linear layers when emphasizing relationships within the information. Use three-dimensional layering to elaborate information and illustrate concepts without switching contexts. Consider opaque layers when presenting elaborative information, and transparent layers when illustrating concepts or highlighting relationships in information.«[8]

The use of the term as outlined above suggests an interdependence of the layers, belonging to each other, being created in a time-based sequence that might be manipulated later.

In the fine arts, layering as a way of arranging paint or collaged elements is commonly practiced, especially when artists are working with physical and narrative elements. Countless examples of the work of painters, sculptors, photographers and writers display a conscious and systematic approach to layering in which context and a broader set of circumstances are incorpo-

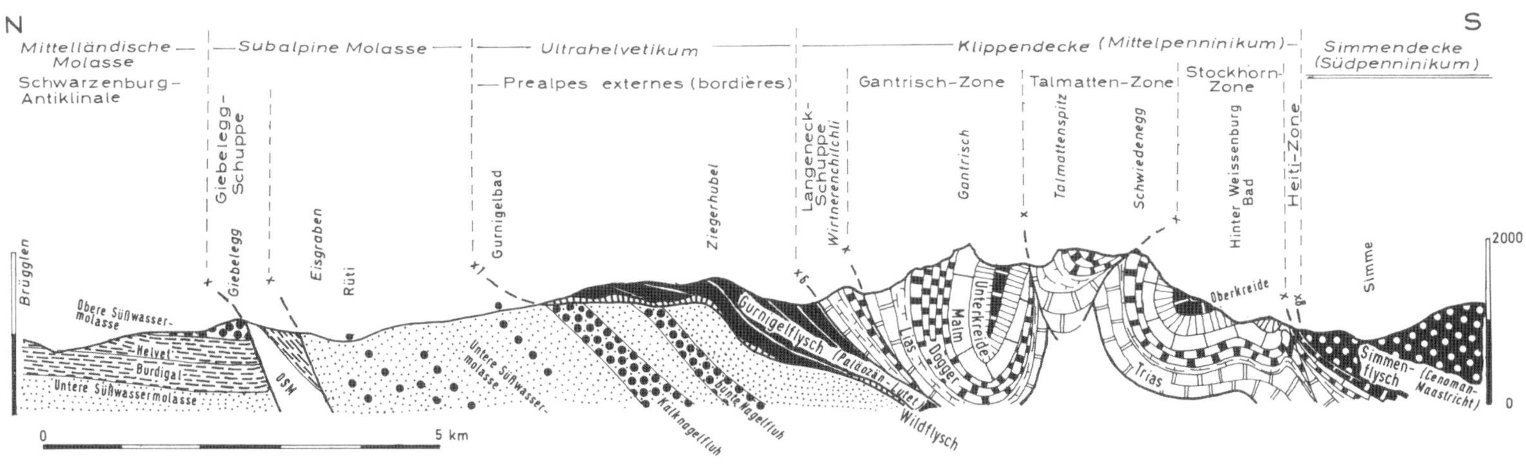

rated into the work. Once more, layering seems ubiquitous but requires definition if used as a conscious strategy. In a discussion of an artistic version of layering, artist and writer Mary Carroll Nelson's essay »Approaching the Layer as a Formal Element and a Significant Metaphor in Art Making«[9] investigates several artists whose work was affected by »Jungian psychology, especially the concepts of the collective unconscious, the anima/animus, and synchronicity«.[10] Nelson calls the protagonists of her theory »layerists« and notes: »The layerists' interest in the continuum of time and space is revealed in a synchronist perspective whereby multiple events or multiple points in space are connected within the layers of their work. As I perceive it, layering is a post-modern approach to artmaking that grows directly from the emergence of a holistic insight within society at large.« She explains further: »Layering is not a style, nor it is limited to either art or craft but affects both.«[11] In the essay, she suggests that the use of multiple layers allows penetration through the first – more recent – layers into the past.

»The artist Robert Smithson at times uses geological terms to describe his sculptural work and writes about »wedges of sedimentary strata«,[12] describing the arrangement of parts and associating his work with the expanded timeframe of the earth's history. Smithson applies the strategy in his sculpture and his writing, finding analogies in the creative process. Sculptures such as *Leaning Strata* (1968), *Shift* (1967) and *Glass Stratum* (1966) exhibit visibly layered planes. As the artist describes one of his glass works: »It's very green, very dense and kind of layered up.«[13] Literally using the images of fossils, Smithson introduces a sense of extreme distant past and an expression of the earth's gravitational force.

Instead of building up layers, Gordon Matta-Clark's work cuts into buildings, exposing material and spatial layering not visible in the intact structure, and breaking the functional surface of rooms into primal spaces seemingly on the verge of destruction. He seems to be acting as the anti-architect but in fact reveals the core of architecture more obviously than the buildings were able to convey without his interventions. Matta-Clark (who studied architecture at Cornell University in Ithaca, New York) describes his process in an interview with a journalist: »At that point [around 1973] I was thinking about surface as something which is too easily accepted as a limit. And I was also becoming very interested in how breaking through the surface creates repercussions in terms of what else is imposed by a cut. That's a very simple idea, and it comes out of some line drawing that I'd been doing. [...] It was the kind of the thin edge of what was being seen that interested me as much, if not more than that, the views that were being created [...] the layering, the strata, the different things that are being severed. Revealing how a uniform structure is established.«[14]

The interest in the edge and the curiosity about what is beneath the top layer leads Matta-Clark to manipulate average buildings into what architects like Carlo Scarpa carefully worked out through their design process. Matta-Clark reveals views that are unexpected, destructive, and informative. In his interest in the layering that lies beneath the established and known object, he is looking for the edge that is testimony to the process of construction.[15]

More recently, the Japanese artist Nobuhiro Nakanishi has worked on showing the passage of time and an ambivalence of the image through his series titled *Layer Drawings*, consisting of images printed on sheets of Plexiglas presented in a spaced assembly.[16] The photos displayed in such multiples create an alternative space and simultaneously represent a sequence of time, as if memory is being visualized.

5. Robert Smithson, *Leaning Strata*, 1968.
6. Robert Smithson, *Shift*, 1967.
7. Robert Smithson, *Mirror Stratum*, 1966.
8. Nobuhiro Nakanishi, *Layer Drawing-Snow*, inkjet print on film, acrylic plastic, 2011.
9. Gordon Matta-Clark, *Conical Intersect*, 27–29 rue Beaubourg, Paris, 1975.

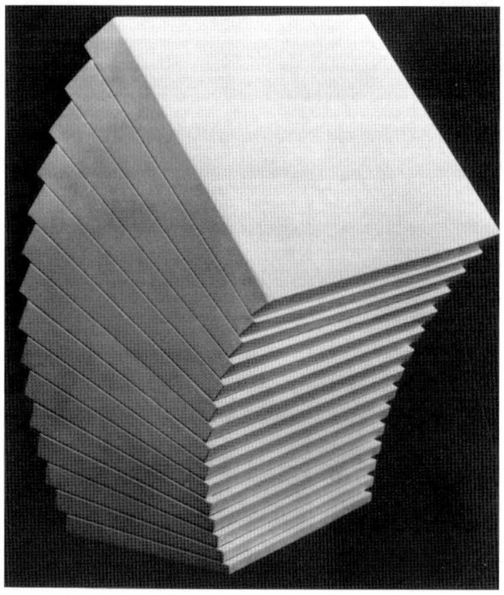

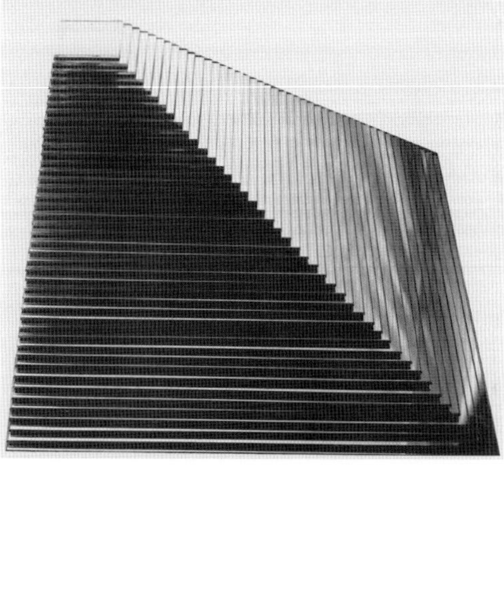

Layering in architecture

Architectural layering involves the realms of time, space, and material. If an important role of architecture is the demarcation of space, the starting point of layering consists of a series of planar elements that constitute skins and spatial separations and that simultaneously speak about their time and cultural content. One or multiple layers of material are necessary to define architectural space. Architectural layers relate to the architectural skin, the façade, surfaces, cladding, and enclosure.

Although the various types of layering are often intertwined and appear in the same project, three types of layering will be discussed: a chronological sedimentation of planes materializing changes over time (temporal layering), the additive sequence of spaces (spatial layering), and the stratification of individual planes (material layering). Even if this text suggests a clear separation of the different types of layering identified, the examples will document that the transition between material and spatial layering is sometimes fluid, and temporal layering in its sedimented configuration can be part of all approaches.

Temporal layering

Like a palimpsest, historic cities frequently reveal temporal layering and aspects of change and intervention over time, a condition familiar to archaeologists who study layer upon layer of remnants of civilization, including architectural remains and urban organization. In historic cities, one can read at least the most recent layers to determine a physical chronology of the city's history; contemporary architects add strata of the 21st century. Cities are composed of several layers that simultaneously display what was built at different times, offering a complex understanding of time in which a view of the present includes the perception of the past. For example, Heinrich Schliemann documented the layers of the historic site of the city of Troy, where he peeled back layer after layer, documenting different historic time frames. The archaeological layers of the city of Rome can be viewed throughout at locations such as the Forum Romanum, which lies below the level of contemporary Rome and offers a sense of the chronological buildup of settlement. Leon van Schaik confirms this view: »Intuitively we all know that architecture grows in cities – which are all tangible manifestations of the mental space of their citizens, buildings superimposed in layers by generation after generation. If in our mind's eye we were to imagine a time-lapse record of a city's growth through the centuries, we would see spaces being formed by jostling ranks of buildings.«[17]

At a larger scale, temporal layering can be observed in urban views that show the overlaying of different plans or maps as they evolve over time. At a building scale, layers can be multiple elements of walls, the skin, the structure, decorative and narrative elements, or part of the spatial composition. Just as the position and order of geological strata contain information related to their age, formation, and origin, the position and form of architectural layers come with information about their function, intellectual scope, and provenance. The possible elements of such an architectural strategy include materials, light, water, and color as well as associations, memories, and analogies embedded in the layers or in the voids between them. The simultaneous perception of different layers is similar to listening to an opera, an experience that encompasses voices and instruments as well as story – the simultaneous reading of the parts and their meaning.

Vittorio Gregotti looks at the impact of technology on architecture history and discusses how different design techniques seem to merge over time when several architects contribute to the same building. Stating that the layers do not necessarily remain legible, he writes, »A very special but frequent case is a work of architecture constructed over a long time that displays the layered work of different architects at different moments, thus turning it into a repertory of diverse techniques that today, with historical distance, we see as completely amalgamated if not homogeneous.«[18]

The principle of layering is testimony to the passage of time and illustrates a sequence of creation. The sequence of elements is not necessarily linear but is nevertheless often readable, allowing for a didactic explanation of how individual layers came together and changed over time. Layers co-exist without a required hierarchy; individual elements, influenced by their neighboring strata, form a complex whole without a specific focus point. Layers can reflect a link between material and message representing a universal whole.

10. Diagram of urban layers densifying over time.
11. Diagram of space defined through separate two-dimensional planes.
12. Diagram of monolith.

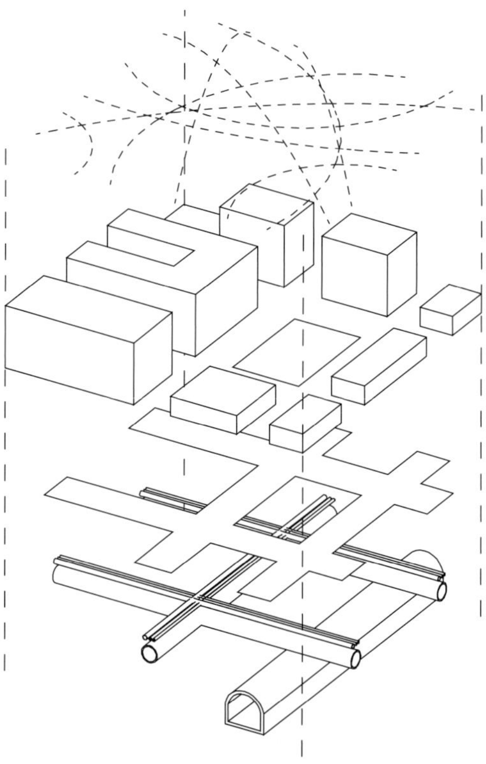

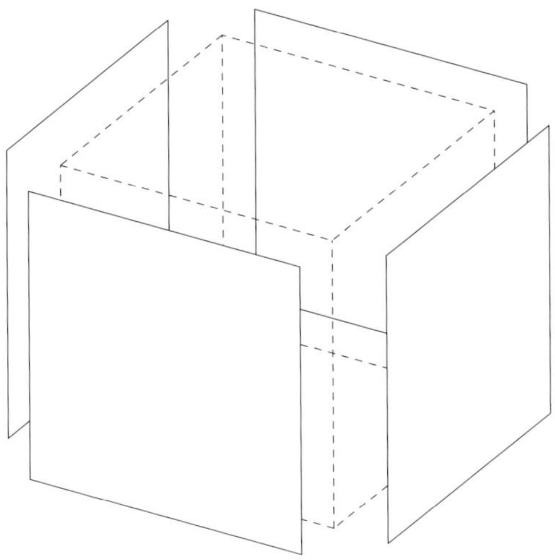

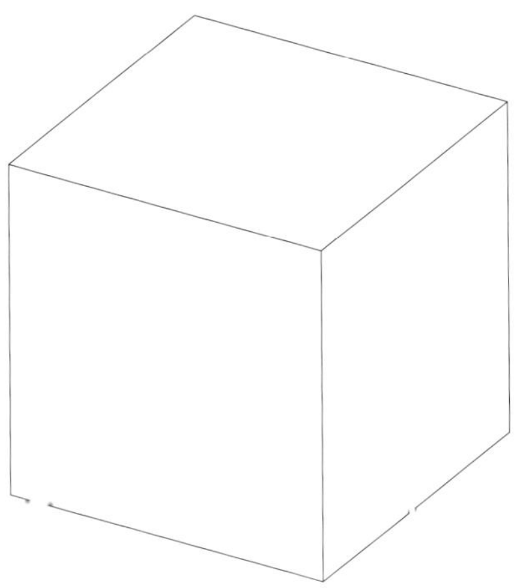

Spatial layering

The separation of spatial and material layering is going to remain opaque in many projects – both are frequently present in the same building, especially in instances where the wall becomes inhabitable and the boundaries between space and enclosure are blurred.

The German theorist Jürgen Joedicke defines (architectural) space as »something enclosed by planar surfaces. This general layman's understanding of architectural space indicates that one has to distinguish conceptually between two elements if one wishes to comprehend the phenomenon of space. These elements are space itself and a spatial demarcation. The fact that space is not identical with its confining elements, in other words with wall, floor and ceiling, seems obvious, for space is defined as the thing existing between these surfaces. Another definition of space as the ›thing between‹ does not exist for the moment.«[19] Joedicke also explains how spatial perception is based on individual processing and cultural formation resulting from a »common tradition or education«.[20] Space is defined by its physical demarcation (even if partial) and the human reading of space based on the experience of occupying it. The physical demarcation is created by the wall and the roof or the overall skin. Corresponding to Joedicke's definition of architectural space, Dom van der Laan defines architectonic space as what is happening in-between the walls: »Architectonic space offers us both limited mass and limited space, in its walls and the space between them.«[21] He describes further how space is related to the enclosure: »Because the space is dependent on the wall, the form of the space can as it were lie alongside of that mass, despite the fact that both forms owe their existence to the formlessness of their immediate environment. The key to this is that the form of the mass arises from the mutual correspondence of opposed surfaces while the form of the space arises from the mutual correspondence of the opposed forms of the wall. Architectonic space makes natural space habitable by coming into being in its midst; the form of the wall makes architectonic space visible by marking it out.«[22]

Although architecture is hollow by nature – providing habitable space of different dimensions – not all architecture expresses its nature as a container. Rodolfo Machado and Rodolphe el-Khoury address the topic of monolithic architecture and its »necessary hollowness«:[23] In much of monolithic architecture, the representational elaboration of the »monolithic« is carried out along and across the limit between the interior and the exterior. »Monolithic Architecture«, we may say, is concentrated in the thickness of the envelope, in the surface.[24]

In the following, the authors distinguish the monolith from concepts such as Venturi's »decorated shed« because the distinction between space and skin in the monolith does not exist. They speculate that monolithic architecture is closely related to industrial design, where the object is at the center of exploration and with that the enclosure is designed to »contain the internal complexity within a compact and hermetic package that has a recognizable and distinct form«.[25] The monolith is eager to wrap space in its entirety, concealing any joints, while layered systems act out their section and visualize the overlap. Both Machado and el-Khoury acknowledge the surface as an »autonomous architectural system«[26] that became responsible for wrapping »more or less complex programs into one package«.[27] They further describe curtain walls of the 20th century: »The surface may be hard, polished, and highly reflective. It may have a discernible thickness in the texture of the revetment and even greater physical depth in the layering of more or less transparent cladding membranes. But the ambition is the same: to endow surface with depth, literal or phenomenal.«[28]

Spatial layering in architecture contrasts the monolithic approach and takes advantage of the space »in-between«, areas separated by a series of zones of different use and atmosphere that allow the simultaneous perception of the areas separated. Spatial layering allows the coexistence of spaces of different character, function, or date of construction. Arrangements can be horizontal, vertical, or concentric, with the axis of the observer frequently being perpendicular to or at least at an angle to the actual spaces or areas. Spatial layering can be used horizontally in plan (following, for example, an organization of increased privacy) or vertically along the section of a building (allowing for different zones of decoration and lighting, especially in spiritual spaces). Horizontal arrangements of spatial layers can create program-related zones that transition into one another, while a vertical arrangement might offer zones of altered lighting and a shift from the human scale to more monumental dimensions (as can be found in religious buildings or spaces).[29] Arrangements of spatial layers can vary geometrically among concentric, parallel, horizontal, or vertical configurations. A moat or multiple walls around a medieval castle constitute spatial layers for defense. Japanese and Chinese pagodas create spatial intensification and concentration above a stupa shielding and marking the relics with a vertical sequence of spaces. Other examples of spatial layering support the generation of connections and simultaneity of rooms or spaces.

In the 18th century, castles and large-scale palaces organized spaces as enfilades, spatial layers that are connected and perceivable through aligned door openings. Traditional Japanese architecture also is highly layered and inspired early modernists looking for ambiguous non-hierarchical spaces that would allow an inclusion of interior and exterior.[30] For example, the Imperial Palace in Kyoto, Katsura, exhibits how space is created through the presence of graphic qualities of lines that articulate modules and elements and through a multiplicity of fixed or mobile planes, openings, and view connections. Proportions are governed by modules arranged along multiple axis systems reaching for compositional balance rather than symmetry. Spatial continuity is achieved through a layered arrangement of planes – a method and mindset also reflected in Japanese painting. Japanese principles enjoyed wide interest in the West – according to Salvator-John A. Liotta, »Frank Lloyd Wright was particularly impressed by the ability of Japanese painters to recreate depth without using perspective. In particular, he got to know and appreciate the work of Utagawa Hiroshige and Katsushika Hokusai, whose work embodies many elements of the Japanese concept of space and layering in particular.«[31]

Don Hanlon uses the central Asian town of Turpan, China, as an example of horizontal layering used to control social relationships: »In the daily life of Turpan we find seven distinct layers of space between the public life of the street and the most intimate family of spaces of a house.«[32] Another arrangement of spatial layers can be concentric, which is frequently seen in religious buildings with central plans such as Brunelleschi's Santa Maria degli Angeli in Florence or the Dome of the Rock in Jerusalem. Hanlon defines layering in this way: »A compelling use of layering is to control social relations. [...] Visitors may penetrate the layers of space to varying degrees depending on their status in relation to the family [...]. In contrast, spatial layering may be devoted to purely aesthetic purposes, as in Rome's Church of Santa Maria in Campitelli. Here the layers of space are entirely for visual effect, an illusion of deep atmosphere and ambiguous scale – an intense theatricality typical of Roman Catholic churches built during the Counter-Reformation in Italy.«[33]

Fumihiko Maki chose the term »oku«, originally used in poetry and painting, to analyze the depth of architectural space and the city – it represents a mysterious and unattainable core. Oku describes not only an inner core but also the experience of approaching the core, which can hap-

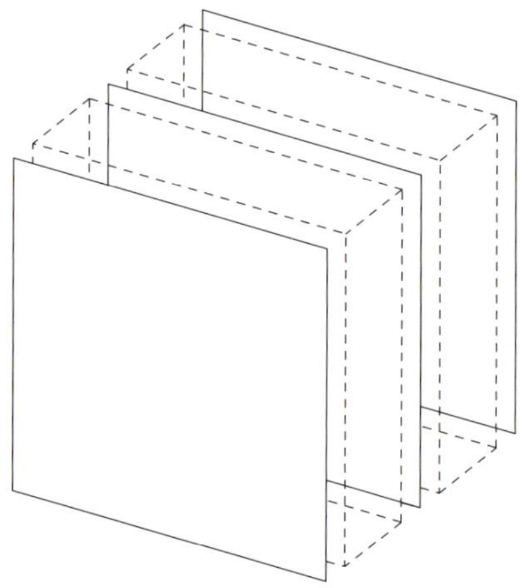

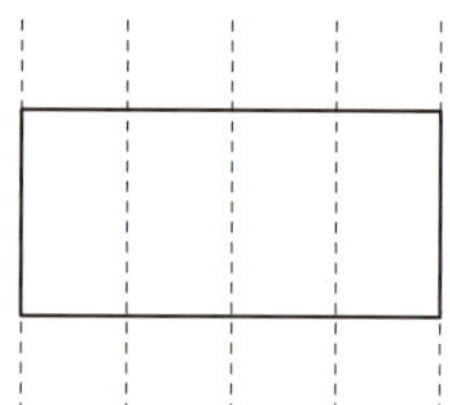

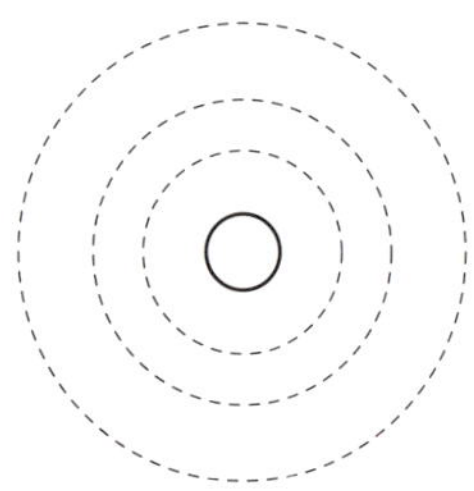

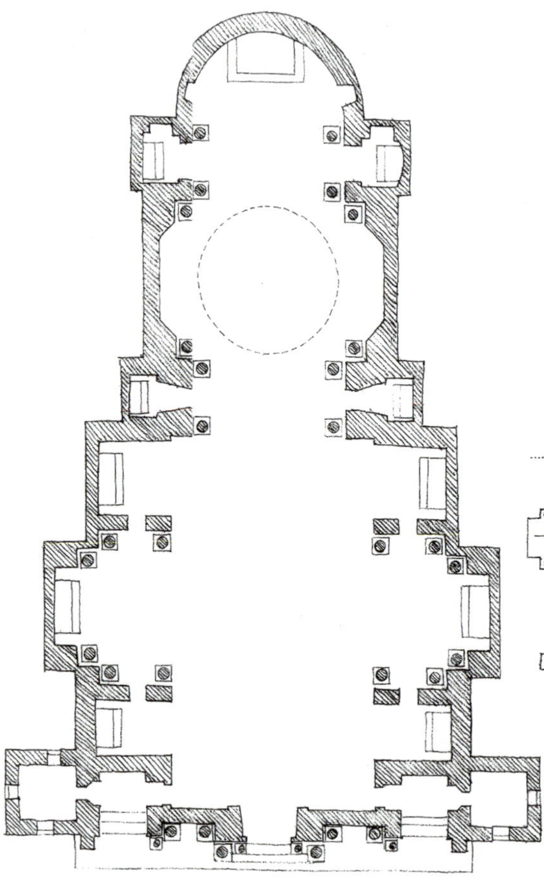

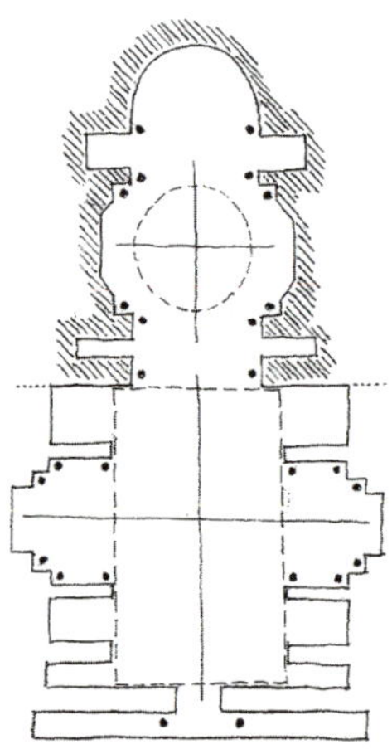

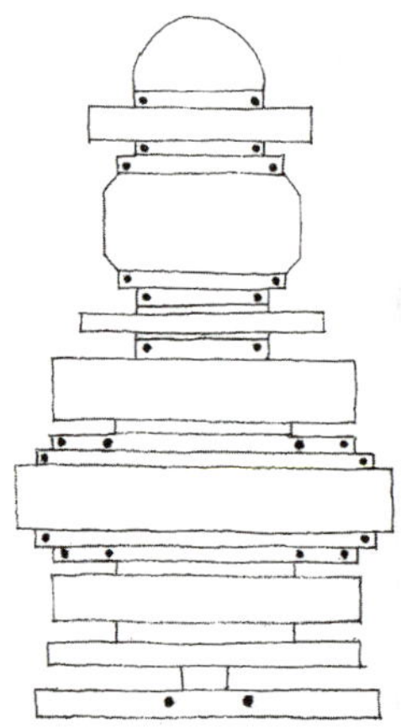

13. Diagram of spatial layering in the church of Santa Maria in Campitelli, Rome.
14. Kiyomizu-dera Pagoda, Kyoto, Japan.
15. Diagram of spatial layering.
16. Diagram of spatial layering arrangements (in plan).
17. Baroque castle Neues Schloss, Tettnang, Germany. Enfilade.
18. Katsura Imperial Palace, Kyoto, Japan. Old Shoin Building, spatial layering.
19. Katsura Imperial Palace, Kyoto, Japan. Ground-floor plan.
20. Diagram of spatial layering of increasing privacy, Turpan, Xinjiang, China.

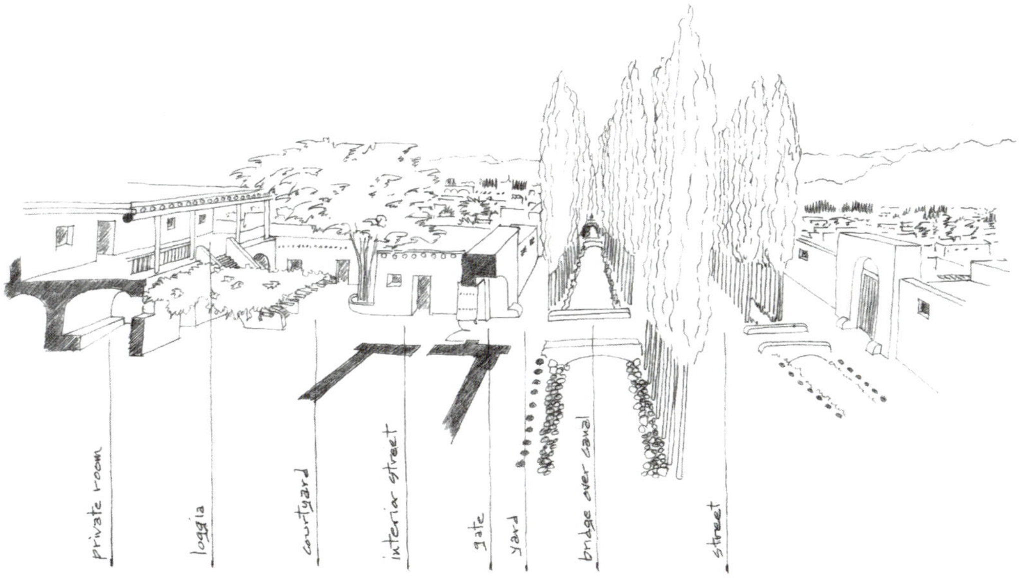

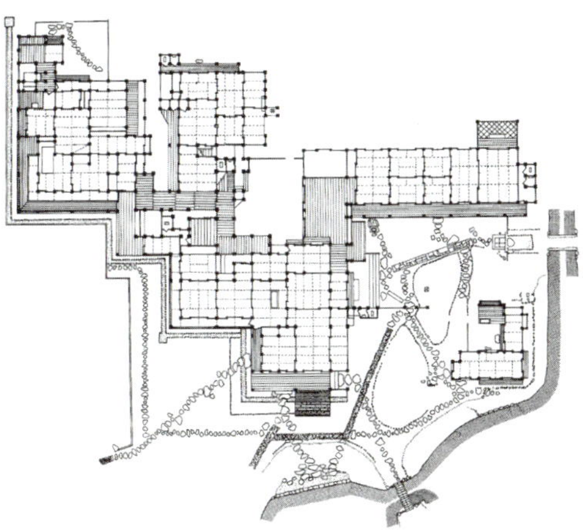

pen through a series of layers. In Maki's own words, »The Japanese have always postulated the existence of what is called oku (innermost area) at the core of this high density space organized into multiple layers like an onion. The word oku, expressing a distinctive Japanese sense of space, has long been a part of the vocabulary of daily life.«[34] For Maki, these types of multi-layered spaces are observable only in Japan, where the depth is generated by an onion-like arrangement of space with an innermost area, the aforementioned oku.[35] Maki writes of the cultural evidence of depth through various disciplines:

»The word oku, expressing a distinctive Japanese sense of space, has long been a part of the vocabulary of daily life, as is evident from such literary classics as the 8th-century anthology of poetry called the Man'yoshu (Collection of Ten Thousand Leaves), the 10th-century Ise monogatari (Tales of Ise), the 14th-century Tsurezureguso (Essay of the Idleness), and kabuki plays of the Edo Period. It is interesting to note that the use of the term with respect to space is invariably premised on the idea of okuyuki, or depth, signifying relative distance or the sense of distance within a given space.«[36]

Matteo Belfiore analyzes the origins of spatial layering in Japan in the book *Patterns and Layering – Japanese Spatial Culture, Nature and Architecture*. He traces its origins in ancient Japanese culture, emerging in painting and in the tradition of Japanese gardens, where depth is created through planes overlaid in varying distances.[37] He connects the mechanics of layering to a strong two-dimensionality, which is used to generate spaces in a way similar to how stage design operates.

In Chinese landscape painting, the depth of a sensory experience can be linked to the existence of multiple viewpoints going hand in hand with the representation of nature as a series of layers extending from foreground to background. Similarly, Japanese garden design can reveal an arrangement of spatial layers in which near objects overlap with those farther away, creating a view of the garden as a whole where the landscape beyond includes the viewer. The overlapping planes act as if framing a theater stage with collapsed layers of landscape elements arranged to emphasize depth and complexity.

Layering is a mechanism that can condense a multitude of information into the skin and wall system used to define contemporary buildings. The masonry wall has turned the vernacular massive masonry wall into a stone veneer. Glass curtain walls constructed of multiple strata have become the norm for many building types. Revealed sectional skins illustrate the thickness and complexity (depth) of the envelope – real or suggested – exposing a possible sequence of several planes in order to form a system emphasizing the interaction of the parts over the singular object. Historic façades often are articulated specifically toward their principal representative side, exhibiting more costly materials and ornamentation on the plane facing the street or a main plaza. The separation of planes can be attributed largely to modern architecture and its predecessors with the intent to break open that box. Arguably the most noted proponent of the approach was Frank Lloyd Wright, who described his strategy of an open plan and spatial freedom in his autobiography and elsewhere.[38] A direct attachment of planes to one another leaving no or little space between qualifies as material layering, which depends on the intent of revealing the built planes.

Material layering indicates the depth of multiple materials and defines zones or sub-spaces within existing spatial realms without the necessity of erecting separation walls. Façades are an obvious place for the use of material layering. A series of different (often planar) elements can be responsible for structural performance, thermal separation, sun protection, waterproofing, information, and ornamentation or decoration. Associative layers allow the narrative of the building and its location to be communicated. As artist and architect, James Wines writes: »Some attention should be paid to the various interpretations and applications of narrative in architecture. On the most obvious level, buildings tell stories when they are endowed with some form of illustrative information. For example, a structure in a politically volatile community might be covered with graffiti or emotionally charged murals. Although these depictions are not intrinsic to the concept of a building, this use of narrative element in relation to architecture is certainly meaningful and valid. There are, however, other methods that are more integral to architecture.«[39]

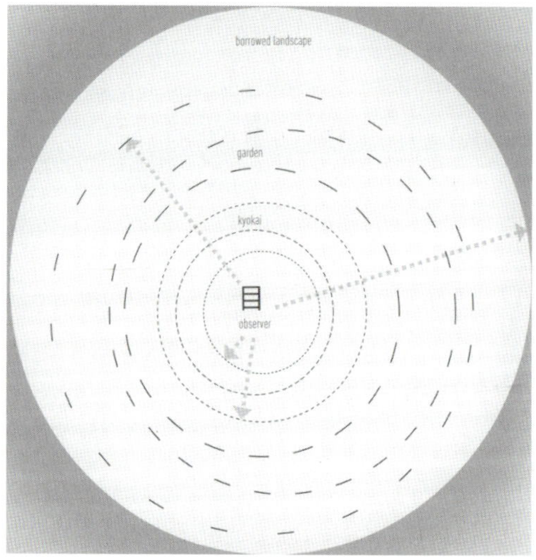

21. Utagawa Hiroshige, *53 Stations* (*Gyosho Tokaido*), Hara, 1840. Framing and spatial layering of views of increasing depth.
22. Diagram by Matteo Belfiore. Japanese design concept of superimposing layers, Suizenji Garden, Kumamoto.
23. Diagram by Matteo Belfiore. Japanese design concept of superimposing layers, Hosokawa Residence, Kumamoto.
24. Katsushika Hokusai, Falls of Kirifuri at Mt. Kurokami, Shimotsuke Province, ca. 1832.
25. Diagram by Matteo Belfiore. Sightlines of an observer in a Japanese house.
26. Diagrams of breaking open the box.
27. Hans Scharoun, Mohrmann House, Berlin, 1939. Axonometric diagram of the interior spatial layering.
28. Hans Scharoun, Mohrmann House, Berlin. Sequence of spatial layering in the interior.

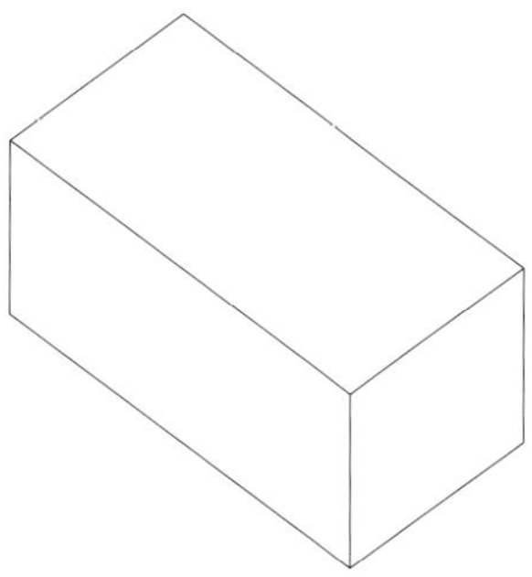

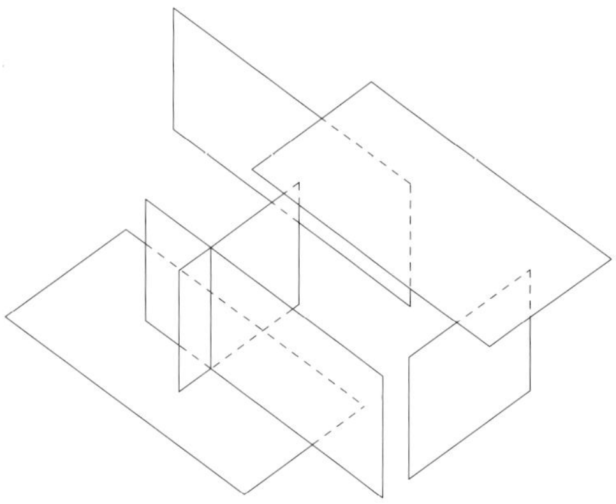

Leon van Schaik writes about »Zaha Hadid's layered mental space«,[40] discussing her winning entry for the Hong Kong Victoria Peak project (1982), in which she »coopted the entire mountain into a Hadid-defined tessellated surface into which the program was slid on small rectangular shelves.«[41] He discusses Hadid's use of layers that appear to fold out of the terrain, integrating implied or real planes of the site into the architecture. Hadid mentions layering frequently in a lecture about her recent work, referring to the building skins broken into several band-like layers as well as interior spaces organized around spatial layering of circulation. She identifies layering as a condition that continues through her entire body of work from Hong Kong's Victoria Peak to the Dong-daemun Design Plaza in Seoul, Korea, which opened in 2014.[42]

In examples of spatial analysis, the term layering is commonly used to describe the succession of spatial sequences. Eckehard Janofske identifies spatial layering in his description of Hans Scharoun's Mohrmann House in Berlin-Lichtenrade (1939):

»A sequence of layers is noticeable when we look through from the dining room in the direction of the window for flowers and houseplants. Apart from the doorlike opening of the room in the direction of the dining area, the buttress between the semicircular dining area and the straight wall of windows in the living-sitting area represents the first layer; the fireplace block is the second. The window behind it, or rather the flower window, is the third and last layer before our eyes are arrested by the landscaping in the garden. It is basically because of this sequence of layers that we have an impression of spatial complexity and distance. As a result of components such as the fireplace block, the surface arch over the sofa, or the masonry pillars between the two spaces that move into our field of vision, the borders of this space are not immediately recognizable, as is the case in a room with four walls.«[43]

In his own house, Robert Venturi applies spatial layering using multiple walls. He describes the house as »a rare manifestation of the idea of a multiple enclosure in my work [...]. It exploits the idea of contrasting spatial layers between the inside and the outside in the series of parallel walls in plan and in the open inner domes supported on diagonal frames in section; the idea of contrapuntal, rhythmic juxtaposition in the relation of the pier openings of the porch, and of the lower and upper windows and of the cupolas above the inner dome, and the idea of a series of spaces en suite which are general in shape and unspecific in function.«[44]

Architect and author Franco Fonatti applies the term layering to Giuseppe Terragni's work. Separating the functions of construction, shell, openings, and shading elements, and shifting them horizontally means that construction is separate from weather protection and causes the elements to appear »layered« because of their additive arrangement. In his analysis of Terragni's Giuliani-Frigerio House, Fonatti separates the façade into four (material) layers. The metal frames of the balustrades form the first layer; the projecting parts, such as the balconies, form the second layer; and the perforated façade forms the third layer. The fourth, innermost, layer is formed by interior parts such as windows and shutters. Fonatti analyzes the agglomeration of the elements, but without ascribing a function to them. The façade creates a transition between inside and outside that gains depth through vertical differentiation.[45]

Toyo Ito intensifies the experience of the horizontal layers of a building's floors in his Sendai Mediatheque, completed in 2001, a glass-clad volume with bundles of columns connecting the vertically stacked spatial layers (that is, floors) of the building, instilling them with views and light. Any multi-story building could be said to stack spaces, but only an act of connecting the spaces visually and functionally would allow that phenomenon to be considered spatial layering.

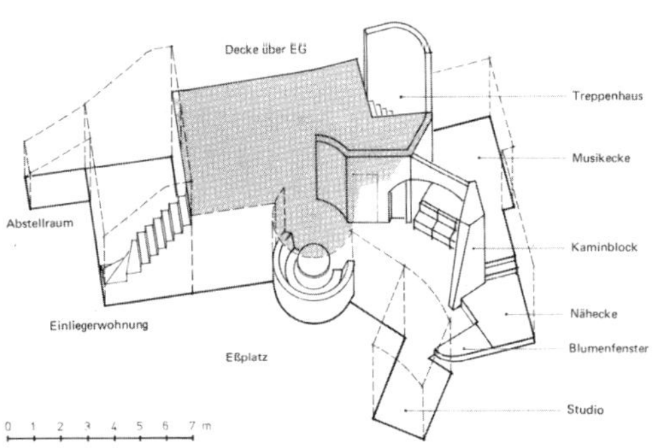

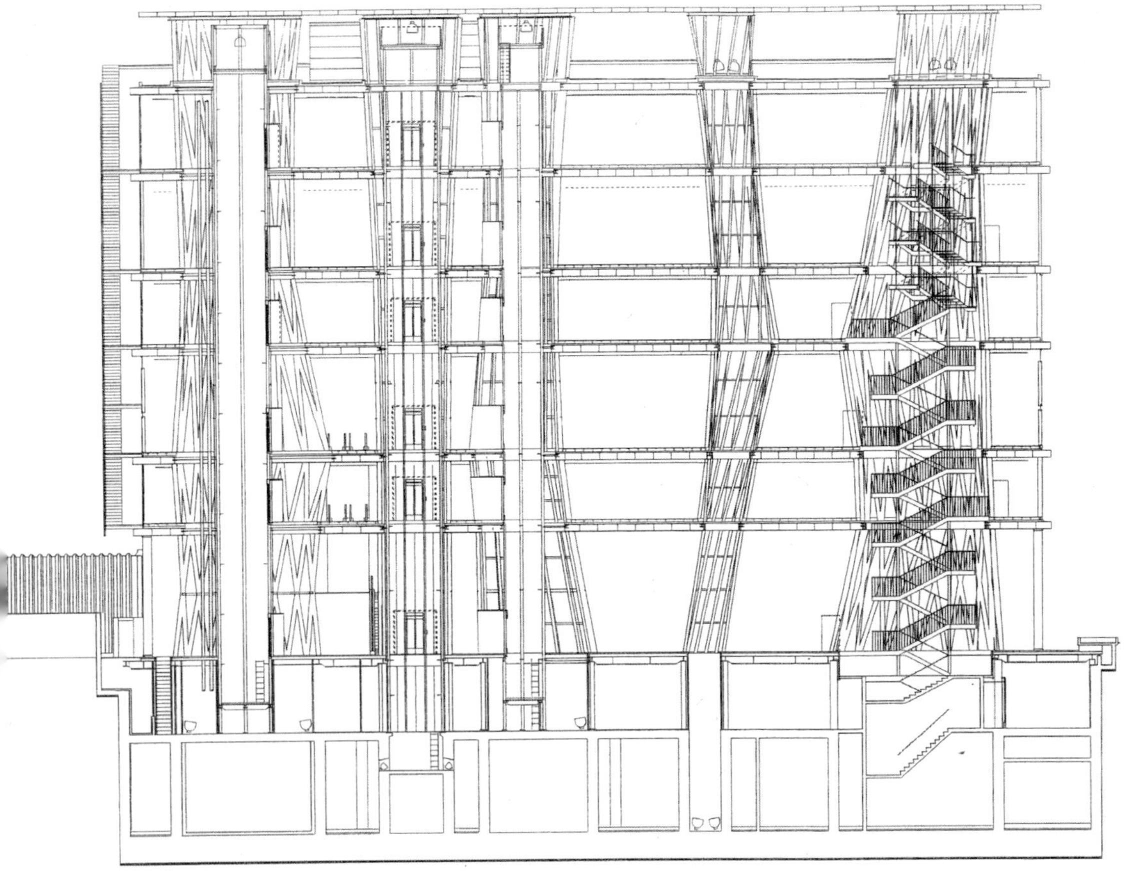

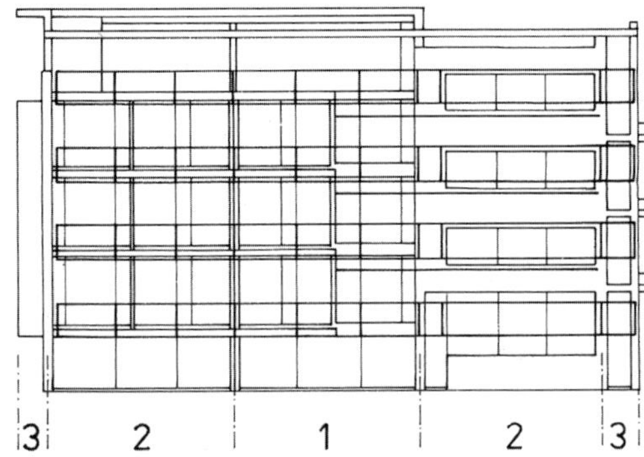
3
2
1
2
3

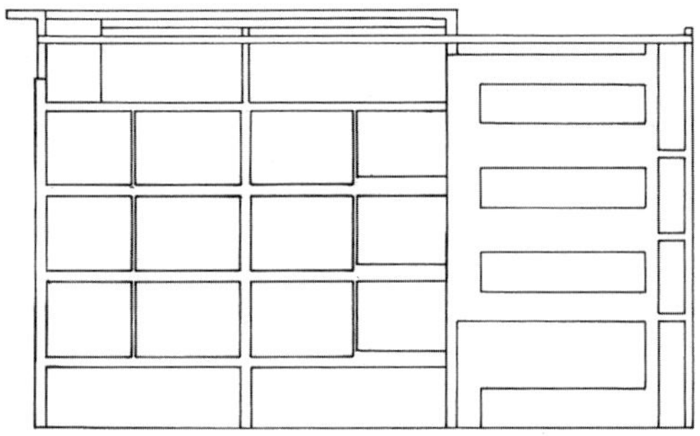

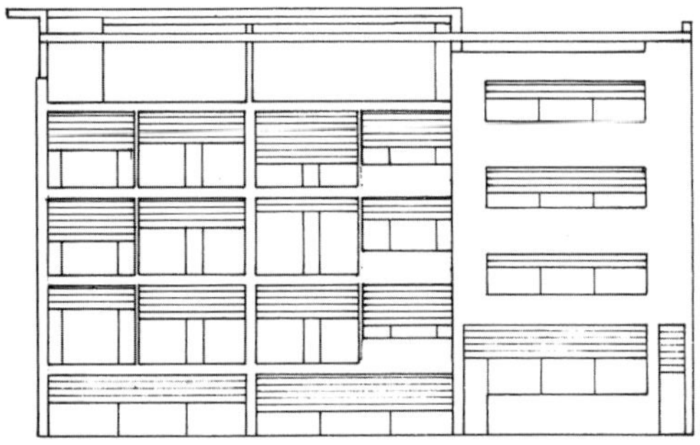

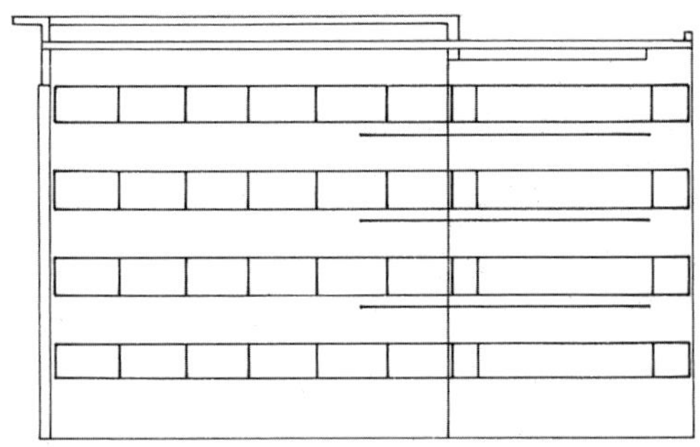

29. Toyo Ito, Mediatheque, Sendai, Japan, 2001. Section.
30. Toyo Ito, Mediatheque, Sendai, Japan. Façade: horizontal layering of the building's floors.
31. Giuseppe Terragni, Casa Giuliani-Frigerio, Como, 1939/1940. Façade.
32. Giuseppe Terragni, Casa Giuliani-Frigerio, Como. Façade analysis of layered elements by Franco Fonatti.
33. Diagram of floor, wall and ceiling elements.
34. Diagram of material layering.

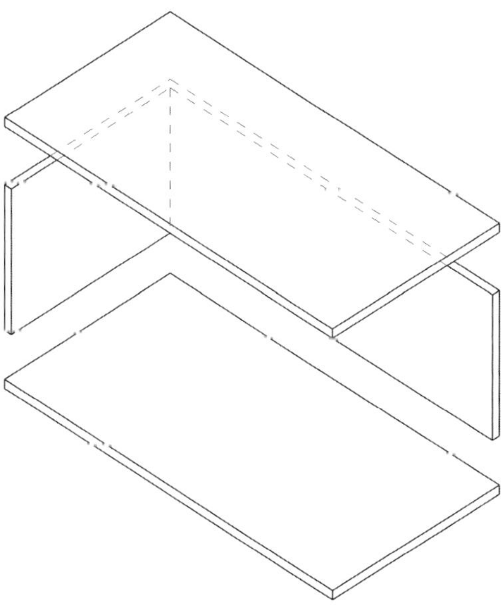

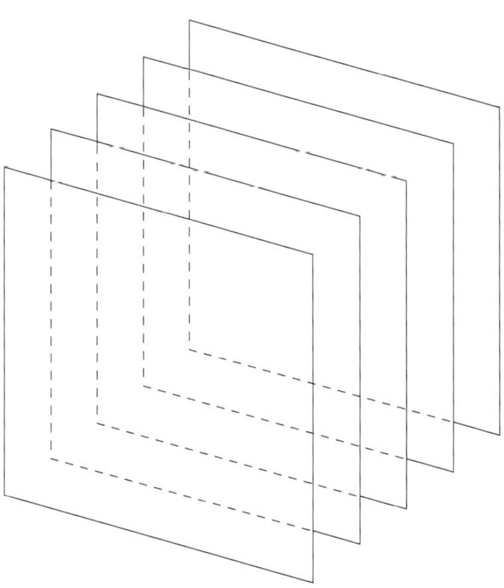

Material layering

Applying the term layering to an individual building rather than an urban fabric can slightly alter its definition. At the scale of a building, layering is based on a perceived separation of spatial enclosures into floor, wall, and ceiling or roof elements and combinations thereof. Individual elements may consist of multiple planes fulfilling a series of specific functions (such as rain screens, optical screens, sun shades, insulating layers, or formal statements and ornamentation). The architectural enclosure can represent the physical wrapper of a building and might transport the structure's narrative, tectonic information, cultural expression, the architect's design intent, and other ideas that might be embedded. The notion of layering understands architectural space as being contained in-between physical boundaries, not distinguishing only between interior and exterior, but also articulating different functions and messages. The curtain wall acts as the building's skin that can be independent from its structural skeleton. A building's planes document its construction process and reflect current society and culture, possibly without the architect's awareness. Layering allows varying formal expressions within one structure altered over time. If layering is viewed as being able to unfold in the physical and informative realm, decoration and advertising become part of the system, and signs and significance exist in addition to the physical structure.

The historically monolithic masonry wall was broken down over the course of time into layers of structure (made from masonry, brick, or being a wood skeleton), cladding or infill (which will be discussed as material layering), and possible elements of sculpture, ornamentation, and communication applied in different thicknesses, real or suggested. Alterations and modifications lead to added layers, stylistic updates, or an emphasis on the parts of a building that are »seen« and thus lead to distinctly visible planes added to existing structures.

The complexity of the façade becomes obvious at openings and points of interaction with light, ventilation, and views. Thomas Herzog writes in the *Façade Construction Manual*: »The composition of multi-layered main façades led to a grand interplay between wall and opening, as in the achievements at the cathedrals in Lucca and Ferrara, where this resulted in three-dimensional façades with all details taking on a sculpted form.«[46] Light and shadows further enhance the notion of depth and complexity expressing superimposition and dynamic forms. Façades are the canvas for decoration and messages on the outer surface that a building, its owner, or the institution it is serving might want to communicate – through sculptural textures or through paintings or other applied two-dimensional graphics.

In his work on surfaces, Joseph A. Amato writes that surfaces »present us with and come as part of wholes, configurations, and contexts. [...] As coverings and epidermises – homogeneous and heterogeneous, permeable and impermeable, permanent and transient – surfaces constitute an immediate and tangible geography of the world and a prima facie index of all its different things.«[47]

Layering relates to elements of the surface, especially at the point where the section is exposed like eroded mountains or incisions into an animal's skin. Architectural and art historians have used the geological metaphor of layering in their descriptions and analytical texts describing the relationship of decoration to the architectural wall. Writing about late Byzantine architecture in Serbia and Thessaloniki, Robert G. Ousterhout describes »the trend from a complex layering of decoration to a simpler, tectonically oriented system«.[48] Material layering in architecture can be defined as the readable sequence of planes, placed or evolved in a way that multiple elements can be read as a system. Different geometric arrangements of layers can be employed, and concentric, horizontal, or vertical compositions can unfold in plan, section, or elevation.[49]

Layers are related to elements such as space, skin, surface, and façade, all potentially made of parts that can overlap and reveal one another. As spatial layering is apparent in the connected room sequences of traditional Japanese architecture or the European Baroque enfilade, material layering evolves around an architectural boundary made from multiple planes. Buildings that undergo changes over time can adopt multiple layers. In such instances, the composition of material layers is defined by the sequence and timing of their placement. Layers can transport the narrative of a built area, and they can act symbolically or illustratively. A formal approach to layering reveals the multiplicity of its objects in section. An exploration of layering involves the analysis of the physical layers, their method of arrangement or evolution, the interstices between the layers, and the embedded narrative. Although much of a façade's materiality might be dedicated to separating an interior from a weather-exposed exterior, articulating transparent and opaque surfaces, another part of it is dedicated to identifying the building with its context through formal and material choices, through a message that is carried through ornament, text, or other media. Formal attributes communicated through an architectural wall or skin have historically communicated the building's or the owner's role and prosperity, an affinity to classic values or other prevalent principles at a time. Communicating different elements in a façade almost automatically leads to layering, obvious, for example, in a building such as the Centre Pompidou in Paris from 1971, where distinctive coloring (blue = air conditioning, green = fluids, yellow = electrical, red = circulation). Times Square in New York further demonstrates the communication of commercial layers, flashing lights, and text as the outer skin of façades. More complex screen-based media façades evolved from that, harnessing light and message, technology and interactivity, to make buildings communicate, advertise and entertain.[50]

The study by architects Robert Venturi, Denise Scott Brown, and Steven Izenour outlined in their book *Learning from Las Vegas* [51] distinguishes a further layer: the symbol separated from the building, a sheet of information, the billboard. Separating symbolic content from the actual building allows this information layer to be explicitly distinct from the architectural volume. In the book, the sign function of buildings is discussed as distinct from the building itself, with the building losing its primary importance. The sign allows the message (or advertisement) to stand separate from the functional volumes. The façade of the building becomes secondary, the billboard offers the narrative, and the building acts as a container. Venturi et al. write about the larger context of Las Vegas: »But it is the highway signs, through their sculptural inflected shapes, and their

35. Urseline Monastery, Landsberg am Lech, Germany, mid-18th century. Layer of paint on façade by Johann Baptist Bergmüller.
36. Diagram of information layer detached from building as billboard.
37. New York, Times Square, 2013. Advertising billboards and façade elements as information layers.

graphic meanings, that identify and unify the mega texture. They make verbal and symbolic connections through associations in few seconds from far away. Symbol dominates space. Architecture is not enough.«[52]

Layering cannot be considered a stylistic tendency; as defined in this essay, layering is an architectural strategy that is legible in many examples of historic and contemporary architecture and urban planning. Only a few examples exhibit a series of planes structured specifically to serve a formal intention. Layering as an approach to design assumes an integrative and sedimentary process in which the individual building or architectural part represents not a final product but a moment in an itinerary of spatial development that integrates site, city, and landscape into the overall design strategy.

The Swiss architect and theorist Pierre von Meiss associates layering with spatial depth, derived particularly from painting. For him, the purpose of layering is the creation of perceived depth even in a shallow arrangement. Von Meiss interprets the use of spatial layers as a phenomenon the purpose of which is to produce the perception of depth, often in conjunction with the representative mechanism of perspective. What is of fundamental importance is that the layers overlap, »since we recognize that an object which partially conceals another is located in front of the latter«.[53] He describes the phenomenon of shallow-depth space achieved by manipulation of planes and transparency: »From the Renaissance until well into the 19th century, painters do not conceal their preference for perspective and spatial depth. Medieval painters and those who paint in a different way, such as Gris, Braque, Le Corbusier, and later Slutzky, are masters of shallow-depth space, in which superposed planes appear crowded and close together. Architects, too, have tried to structure their buildings and spaces by these means. Some, in their work, use the parallel planes, with minimal and undefined intervals between them, not only shallow-depth space, but also applying the phenomenon of transparency created by fragmentary disappearance and reappearance of one plane behind the other. This is the principle of several shallow-depth spatial layers superposed, particularly in the area of the façade, favored by Terragni in the Frigerio House in Como, Le Corbusier in the Villa Stein in Garches, or Carlo Scarpa in the articulation of the walls and windows of the Museo di Castelvecchio in Verona.«[54]

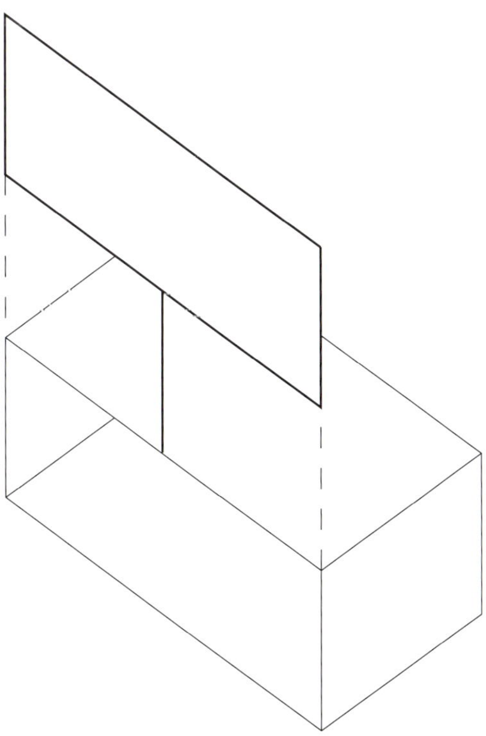

Material layering can correspond closely to the geological and sedimentative content of the term explained above. Unlike spatial layering, which is defined by voids or spaces between multiple planes, material layering consists of planar elements that are arranged on top of each other to form a single element. Layers that are added to walls or surfaces that delineate space can form sub-spaces within them, as can be seen in the exhibition spaces by Scarpa. Cladding forms the outer layer of a wall or architectural separation, usually revealing that there is something else underneath, that the skin and what it expresses is held by something else, once more pointing to the hollow nature of architecture.

38. Carlo Scarpa, Castelvecchio, Verona, 1958 to 1964. Layers inserted into façade and roof.
39. Carlo Scarpa, Castelvecchio, Verona. Glass layer overlaying Gothic fragments.
40. Carlo Scarpa, Castelvecchio, Verona. Caserma Building, ground-floor stucco wall panel creating spaces for exhibited pieces.
41. Carlo Scarpa, Castelvecchio, Verona. Wall cladding at stair: new layer of stucco panels revealing existing wall surface.
42. Carlo Scarpa, Castelvecchio, Verona. Area below Cangrande statue, stone layers inserted as new pavement.
43. Carlo Scarpa, Fondazione Querini Stampalia, Venice, 1961–63. Introduction of new layer added on top of existing stone steps. Detail.
44. Carlo Scarpa, Querini Foundation, Venice. Intro-duction of new layer added on top of existing stone stair.

Technical and performance-related demands expected from building components in façades have led to the separation of individual functions and their expression in a multi-layered façade. Alfred Breukelman, who wrote extensively about the design and performance of the exterior wall, writes: »The resolution of the construction into individual layers, which was carried out intentionally, divided a particular building component into different elements for different functions. Only the totality of the layers makes the wall physically adaptable to divergent climatic conditions.«[55] This type of »variability through layering«[56] helps to optimize the implementation of technical requirements. External weatherproofing layers protect against the elements. A drainage layer behind the weatherproofing layer is followed by insulation against heat and cold between the interior and exterior. Fully glazed skins require additional elements to reduce the impact of solar radiation. Soundproofing might be added, and load-bearing functions might also be located in the façade;

the innermost layer provides vapor barriers and wind-proofing as well as the functional or decorative skin of the interior space.

Double façades frequently are implemented to fulfill present-day technical challenges and energy expectations.[57] The multi-layered wall often involves a double-skin assembly »where an interstitial air pocket is created between two layers of materials – typically glass – [and] the stack effect is driven by solar heat gain«.[58] Technical development does not stop with the separation of building elements according to their function; the goal is the automatic variability of building components that spontaneously adapt to changing conditions. The focal point of this architecture is the variable outer wall that adapts to indoor and outdoor climate, takes into account specific user demands, and at the same time permanently resists physical stress factors, such as weather conditions. The term outer wall, in this context, does not appear to be appropriate for describing such building elements. It actually consists of multi-layered, sensitive thin strata or skins, capable of lightning-speed reaction while their appearance changes continually.[59] The development of the thermally active façade and the layers evolving over time (strongly related to the heating and cooling systems of the buildings in question) are traced by Kiel Moe in his book *Thermally Active Surfaces in Architecture*. Moe diagrams the number of layers in a building envelope and the embodied energy, distinguishing assemblies that follow water-based strategies for heating (and cooling) from air-based thermal strategies.[60] Those strategies also lead to formal properties that read as layered. In addition to allowing air flow and vented wall details, sunshading devices frequently act as yet another layer potentially with photovoltaic elements for energy production.

On a much smaller scale, British architect Mike Davies developed the system of the polyvalent wall in 1981 (while working on the Lloyd's Building with Richard Rogers in London), which once more unites the functions described above into a single element consisting of several micron-thin layers. These individual skins fulfill a number of different requirements and are capable of reacting to changing outdoor conditions. Davies developed what is called the »intelligent façade«, which adapts to prevailing circumstances.[61]

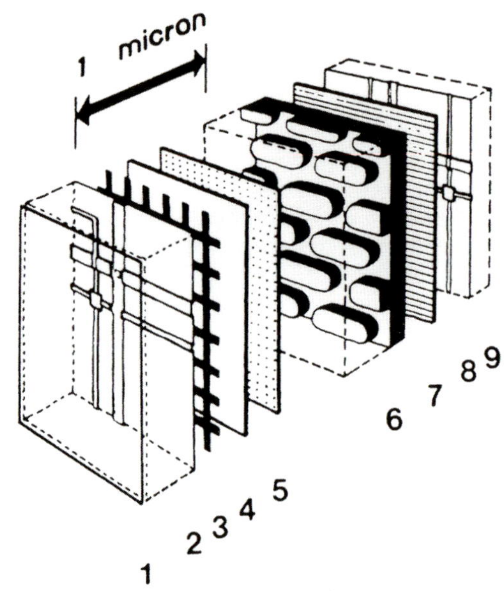

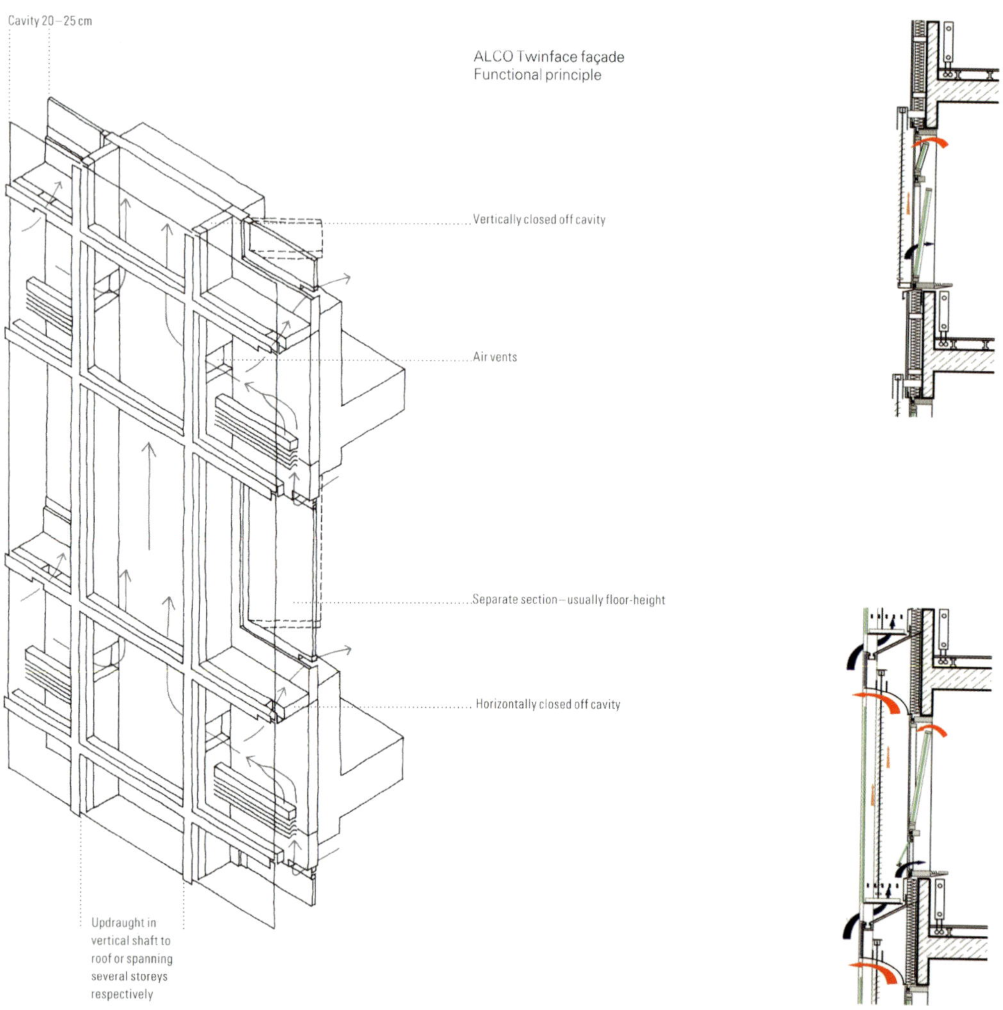

ALCO Twinface façade
Functional principle

45. Klaus Daniels, Alko twinface façade. Axonometric view of façade layers, airflow and operable elements.
46. Diagrams of single-skin and double-skin façade construction.
47. Mike Davies, micro layering within one glass element.
48. Thomas Herzog, photovoltaic canopy in front of supply hall 1 in the commercial zone of south-east Erfurt, Germany, 1999–2001. Section and elevation of multi-layered façade.
49. Thomas Herzog, photovoltaic canopy in front of supply hall 1 in the commercial zone of south-east Erfurt, Germany. Drawing.

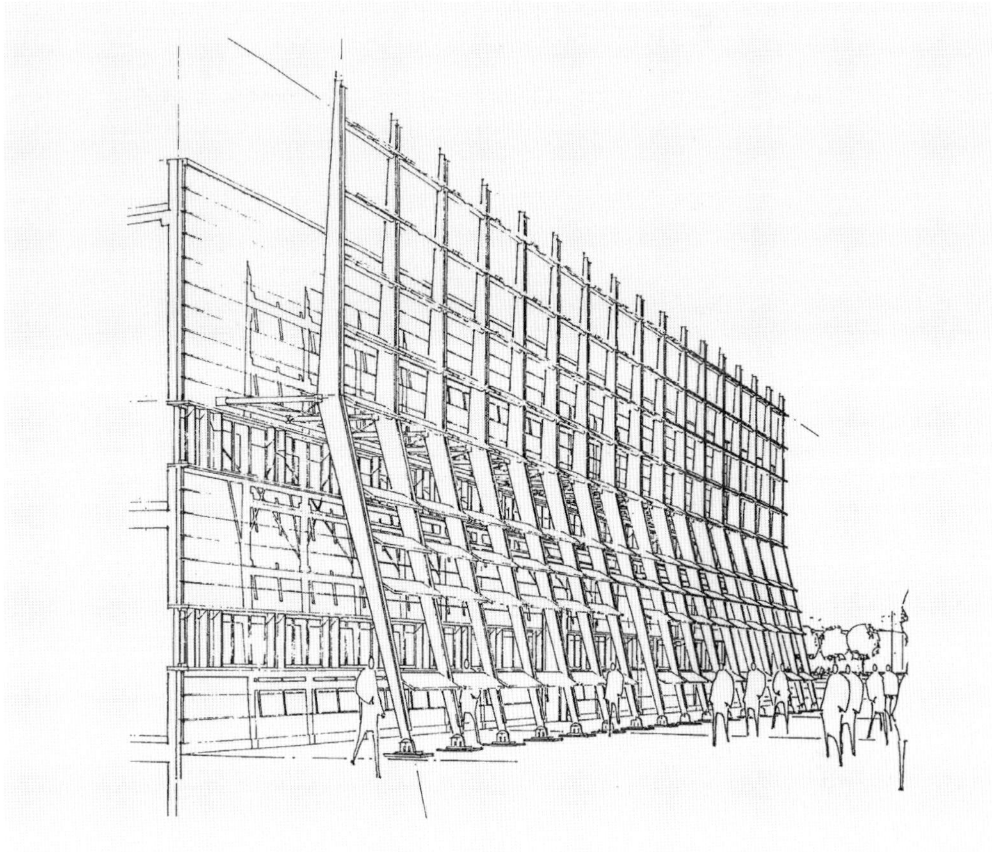

Since the beginnings of the »intelligent façade«, layered façades have been expected to react interactively to a changing micro-climate environment. An intelligent skin is expected to be flexible and dynamically changing, usually in adjustment to energy requirements or glare. What used to happen manually in traditional construction, especially in larger structures, is complemented by a capacity for automatic change, adjustments based on measurements and a built-in reaction. An analogy with the human skin is difficult to avoid, where a complex system of layers fulfills an incredible feat of thermal control and adaption. As Michael Wigginton and Jude Harris write in their book *Intelligent Skins*, »The human skin is a good model for how we would like the building skin to behave. It adapts to temperature and humidity, can feel a breeze or the slightest touch, and can repair itself. It is waterproof and yet permeable to moisture.«[62]

Living walls take the performance of façades further, going beyond energy gains or performance and contributing to the air quality of the surrounding context. One example among many façades that do more than provide separation between interior and exterior is the living wall (Active Phytoremediation Wall System) developed by the Center for Architecture Science and Ecology (CASE) at the Rensselaer Polytechnic Institute in collaboration with Skidmore Owings and Merrill (SOM). It houses plants in a modular arrangement of containers. The system operates as an air-cleaning utility by sending air from the interior spaces to travel through the roots and rhizomes of the plants and then re-introducing it to the interior environment.[63]

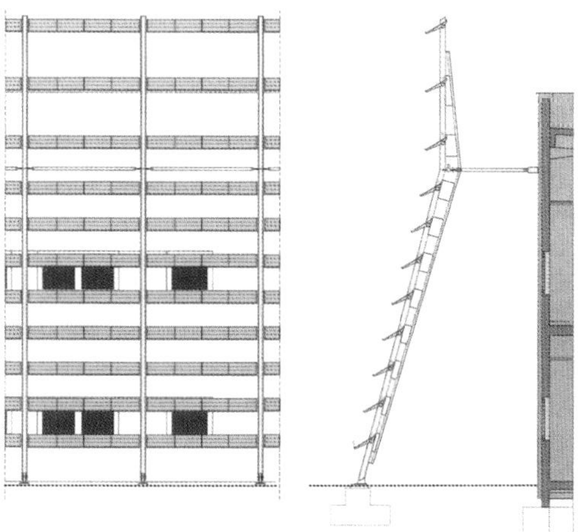

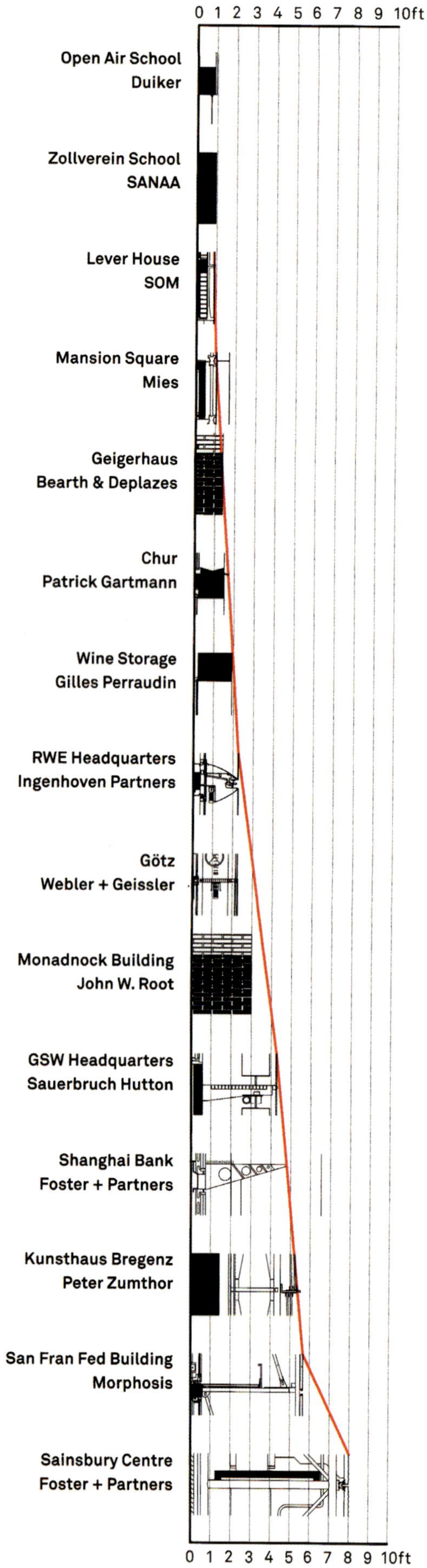

Effective depth

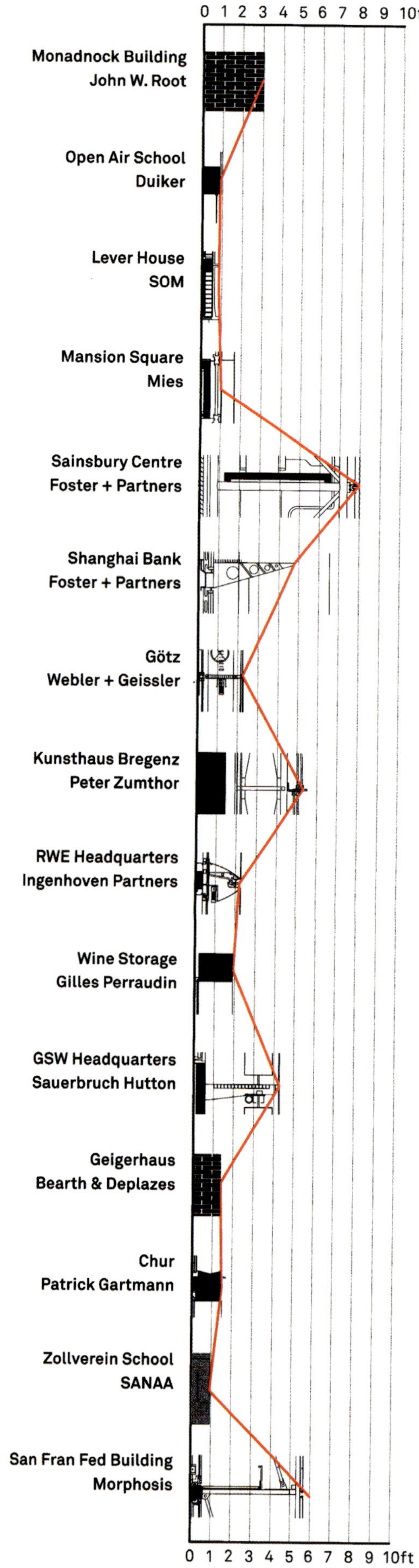

Chronological

50. Kiel Moe, diagram of thermally active layers within façades throughout history. Number of layers and depth.
51. Diagram of ancient Roman masonry-wall construction.
52. William Le Baron Jenney, Fair Store, Chicago, 1891. Steel frame construction.

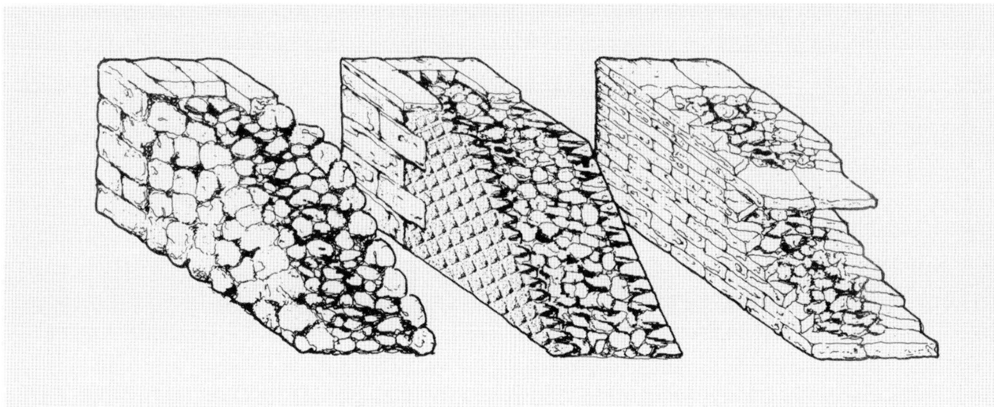

A history of layered architecture

Vitruvius describes how the Greeks built solid walls while the Romans separated the wall into its outer layers and facings and inner fillings. »But our workmen«, he writes, »in their hurry to finish, devote themselves only to the facings of the walls, setting them upright but filling the space between with a lot of broken stones and mortar thrown in anyhow. This makes three different sections in the same structure; two consisting of facing and one of filling between them. The Greeks however, do not build so; but laying their stones level and building every other stone lengthwise into the thickness, they do not fill the space between, but construct the thickness of their walls in one solid and unbroken mass from the facings to the interior.«[64] Economy and formal expectations for the outer layer and formal expression of the façade play equal roles in the subsequent development of the architectural enclosure wall.

The historian Ulrich Pfammatter describes the history of building construction as »the tendency to dissolve mass«.[65] He documents the liberation of the façade, its shift from partition to skin. As examples, he cites how Leon Battista Alberti articulates the »dissolution of the wall as conceptual, design and construction task«[66] and how a subtle layering defines Alberti's façade for the Palazzo Rucellai in Florence. »The structuring of the wall as a load-bearing ›skeleton‹ that follows the internal layout of the rooms, as well as intermediate layer of leftover pieces of stone, described as ›supplements‹, between the inner and outer ›incrustations‹ anticipates new terms such as ›building structure‹ and ›economy of construction‹. Within the wall layer ›stone piers‹ served ›to carry

the layer of beams‹«, Pfammatter writes.[67] He traces the layering of the wall that led from the Renaissance to Modernism, stating that »Alberti thus introduced the tradition from the homogeneous wall to the structured and layered wall in terms of both theory and practice, whereas in Gothic buildings this development occurred as a result of ›necessity‹. The differentiation between load-bearing and non-load-bearing elements as well as the way the wall is built up in layers anticipates the industrial era and Modernism, as manifested by, for example, Mies van der Rohe's ›skin and bone‹ approach.«[68]

In the 18th century, Jean-Nicolas-Louis Durand's school developed a virtual grid to replace the stone-based system of the classical orders. Auguste Perret experimented with a reinterpretation of French masonry construction in concrete while slowly dissolving the wall into layers at the same time. Discussing an early separation of frame and infill in Perret's work, the architect Amy Gardner writes, »This secondary frame is part of the trumeau, whose identity is ambiguous. Structurally (the façade of the Musée des Travaux Publics), it acts as a concrete frame. Representationally, it is a masonry wall. The ambiguity of the actual element parallels the ambiguity inherent in the 18th-century definition of trumeau. This ambiguity in Perret's trumeau also suggests a curtain wall assembly. His detailing of the trumeau indicates that this building is monolithic and layered.«[69]

Technology developed during the Industrial Revolution enabled the efficient separation of iron frames and masonry skins. Materials shifted from cast iron to milled steel and thus opened many more possibilities to the skin and skeleton principle in architecture. This development led not only to the industrial buildings in Great Britain and France but also fostered the evolution of the early Chicago skyscrapers with their steel frame structures and early versions of the modern curtain wall in terracotta. Standardized construction was pioneered in the early 19th century in England, with William Strutt's Calico Mill in Derby exhibiting an iron structural skeleton wrapped by the exterior wall. Infill panels and iron-framed windows appeared in combination with pier construction in the Stanley Mill in Stonehouse from the early 19th century, announcing the »complete dissolution of the wall [...] the transforming step towards the curtain wall«.[70] The notion of the free façade was of interest to many architects during the modernist period. Le Corbusier lists the »free façade« in his *Five Points for a New Architecture*,[71] which enabled a continuing series of buildings to follow the earlier modern buildings in Germany and the Netherlands.

The polychromy debate

As important as the structural potential of steel skeleton systems emerging out of the Industrial Revolution was the realization that paint had been used on the exteriors and interiors of ancient Greek temples. The discovery of a previously unknown thin layer of paint as the outer skin of antique temples at the end of the 19th century resulted in a controversy among scholars, archaeologists, and architects regarding the true nature of classic architecture. The idea of ancient Greek temples as pure monolithic structures had to be revised, together with the related perception of simplicity and clear architectural expression. The addition of paint over stone suggests a division in structural and communicative layers that ties together structure, spatial definition, and ornamentation, thus associating mass and message.

The polychromy debate[72] goes back to sculptor Quatremère de Quincy (1755–1849), who was the lifelong secretary of the Académie des Beaux-Arts in Paris and is said to have been the first to use the term polychromy, in the context of a conference at the Institut des Beaux-Arts in 1806. In his research, Quatremème de Quincy investigates the use of color in ancient Greek sculpture, publishing his findings in 1814 under the title *Jupiter Olympien: ou l'art de la sculpture antique considéré sous un nouveau point de vue; ouvrage qui comprend un essai sur le goût de la sculpture polychrome*.[73] Discussing sculptural work, he refers to the existence of additional layers of color on the monumental statue of Jupiter in the Temple of Olympia. In 1833, Quatremème de Quincy also published a dictionary of architecture in which he develops definitions for major architectural concepts and their application. »Incrustation«,[74] for example, is defined as a metal coating used by goldsmiths, furniture-makers, and architects. »Façades«[75] according to Quatremème de Quincy, are subject to different stylistic treatments depending on their structural purpose. He sees structure as the vehicle that carries the poetic language of architecture, comprising beauty of form and proportions. In contrast stands the term construction, which comprises static, technical, and material-related features. In the initial stages, however, his observations in the realm of polychromy relate to large-scale Greek sculpture.

53. Antoine-Chrysostôme Quatremère de Quincy, reconstruction of Jupiter Olympien. Colored drawings showing layers of paint on statue and interior of the temple.
54. Jakob Ignaz Hittorff, *Restitution du temple d'Empédocle à Sèlionte ou l'architecture polychrome chez les Grecs*, Paris, 1851. Frontispiz. Colored drawing showing colored architectural elements.

German-born French architect Jakob Ignaz Hittorff (1792–1867) spent extended periods of time in Sicily and in 1830 published colored renderings of ancient buildings. He presented his findings at a lecture titled »Memoire sur l'architecture polychrome chez les Grecs« at the Académie des Inscriptions in Paris. He was highly involved in publicizing the ancients' love of color, contributing to a re-definition of the essential ingredients of architecture.[76] »For Hittorff«, Hanno-Walter Kruft writes, »color is a means of protecting the material and therefore, in his eyes, something that needs to be used with greater justification in contemporary Paris than in ancient Athens.«[77]

Auguste Choisy (1841–1909), in his *Histoire d'Architecture*, presents a history of building based on construction technology »that traces back the complexity of all architecture to a few simple lines«.[78] This comprehensive history describes the »continuity of a technological development«[79] and deals almost exclusively with construction-related and technical characteristics of various periods. In addition to providing a technical analysis, Choisy addresses the aesthetic expression of architectural elements and their proportions. »Stylistic developments, for him, are nothing but the expression of new methods of construction«, according to theorist Hanno-Walter Kruft.[80] Choisy's study divides architecture into its elements; thus, he devotes separate chapters to construction, form, proportion, and decoration. Although he keeps decoration and construction separate, he examines the various epochs of the history of construction. His study of Greek architecture, for example, shows layers of paint or material being used to cover the structures. Choisy writes, »The custom of covering the stone with a layer of ceramics was the result of a tradition from a time when inadequate tools made it difficult to cut the edges of stone blocks in a regular way.«[81] Choisy traces the need for a decorative layer back to the lack of available stonecutting tools and thus defines it as a means of regulation and leveling. The outer layer can make the construction stand out and elucidate it, he states, and mentions Hittorff's proof that the Greek monuments were painted.[82]

Henri Labrouste (1801–1875) spent the years from 1825 through 1829 in Italy. With the use of watercolors, he visualized an Etruscan-influenced architectural image of a pre-classical world. Like Hittorff, Labrouste tried to extract practical conclusions from his investigations, apparent in his Bibliothèque Sainte-Geneviève, built between 1845 and 1851 in Paris. The façade contains »reminiscences of many other things he had admired, such as Wren's library in Cambridge, Alberti's Tempio Malatestiano in Rimini, Michelozzo's Banco Mediceo in Milan, and Sansovino's Library of San Marco in Venice. This distillation of knowledge, which we have also found to be at the heart of the work of Felix Duban, was, however, considered to be Labrouste's great contribution.«[83] From a »distillation of knowledge«, Labrouste extracts a layer of association that conjures up narrative elements, reminders of past examples with which to associate. In addition to emphasizing the protective function that stucco and paint might have for stone, Labrouste interacts intensively with decorative functions, regarding which Hanno-Walter Kruft states: »On principle, Labrouste makes a distinction between a building's structural framework and the exterior decorative form – though he would like the forms of decoration to be determined by the construction and the material.«[84] Karl Hammer brings the polychromy discussion to a point: »In the German-speaking part of Europe, Gottfried Semper continues to move in this direction. At this point architecture is transformed from a monolithic into a many-layered structure whose background can be provided by functional, cultural, and aesthetic aspects.«[85]

In 1935, the German architect Franz Kugler (1808–1858) published a book examining polychromy. He believes the layers of color are reduced to individual ornamented parts of Doric temples, such as the frieze above the main ledge. »In all other methods of construction used in the ancient world that consist of pillars and horizontal lintels«, he writes, »the crowning main ledge is located directly above the architrave: it is only in Greek architecture that a third section is inserted between the two – the frieze, whose purpose is perfectly described by its name, zophorus, ›that which bears the images‹. It is used to give the building a worthy sculptured ornamentation, which would have nullified the laws of architectonic form in the building's lower parts.«[86] Layers in the form of paint, according to Kugler, serve a clear purpose and must be used only in illustrative areas of the building. The ornamented sections convey information, indicate the importance and cultural position of the building, or clarify the form and contour of individual parts of the architecture. Regarding the use of color in architecture, Kugler writes: »For the special characteristic nature of those components that have a curved profile is not easy to recognize, particularly when they are continued in longer lines; the eye is more apt to notice the effect of the shadows (which, by the way, can only be effective when the lighting is favorable) than the line of the profile. In order to make the line clear to the eye in every section of the component, it was ornamented with color, reproducing that very profile in its main lines – though incidentally appearing to be freely designed in an artistic way.«[87]

He further describes the addition to temples of ornamentation symbolizing victory: »Of several temples we know that the architrave or frieze was decorated with gilded shields that were generally consecrated by lucky victors from the spoils of victory. Well-known are the twenty-one shields that adorned the temple of Jupiter in Olympia – the votive gifts of Mummius; in the same way, the temple of Apollo in Delphi was ornamented by the Athenians after the Marathon victory, and the Aetolians after the victory over the Gauls. On the Parthenon in Athens you can still see here and there the holes of the clamps in the architrave and round markings with a roughly 3-1/2-foot diameter, clearly indicating that a similar ornamentation was used.«[88]

This discovery and acceptance of layers of paint in ancient architecture promoted normative studies in architectural theory that discuss the tectonic repercussions of separating decoration and narrative intent from the constructively necessary structure. Karl Bötticher (1806–1889) worked extensively on the tectonic mechanisms of Hellenistic Greece. The Hellenists' way of placing structural elements, according to Bötticher, corresponds with the principle of the creative power of nature. The content of each building is expressed in its form. The result is a set of laws that are »high above the arbitrariness of the working subject«.[89] Bötticher's understanding of tectonics separates buildings into two major components, the core form and the art form. This separation is not about separating construction and shell, but rather about a mechanical component that fulfills required functions (core form) and a decorative component (art form) that clarifies functions and »symbolizes the essence of the components«.[90] Bötticher explicates these two forms in detail in the following passage: »The core form of each component is the mechanically necessary, the statically functioning pattern; the art form of each component on the other hand is only the characteristic of explaining the function. […] However, this characteristic does not merely symbolize each component's particular essence, but also the way it is related to the adjoining components; it also contains the juncture of those working together with it; and just as all components are already mechanically joined in a static whole, the joining symbols figuratively link all components logically into one inseparable organism. This explanatory characteristic is therefore only a shell of the component, as it were, a symbolic attribute of the latter – decoration. It comes into being at the same moment that the mechanical schema of the component is conceived: the idea of both is one, they are both born together.«[91]

According to Bötticher, the outer layer or characteristic attribute that accompanies the core form has no material or structural function to fulfill. It has an ethical purpose to represent the structural function that the core by itself takes care of physically – symbolizing that very same content. The outer layer carries out what the core performs; it comments and symbolizes in metaphorical ways what the actual core form does.[92]

The German theorist Heinrich Hübsch (1795–1863) defines architectonic beauty as the equivalent of a core and an art form working together harmonically: »Let us, then, venture to say it: perfect beauty is virtually a deep fusion of the above-named two sides, whose most extreme characteristics are exactly each other's opposites, and that its two sides, whose most extreme characteristics are exactly each other's opposites, and that its dialectical life arises precisely from the

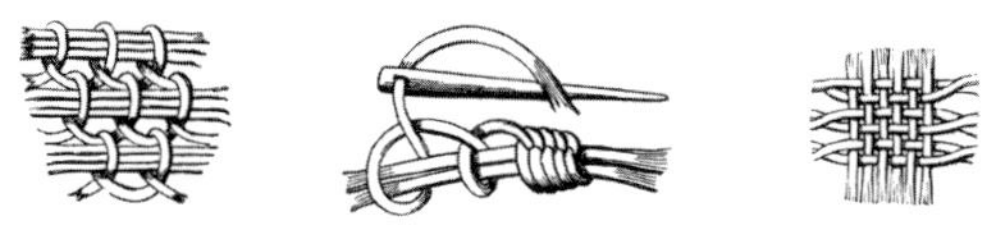

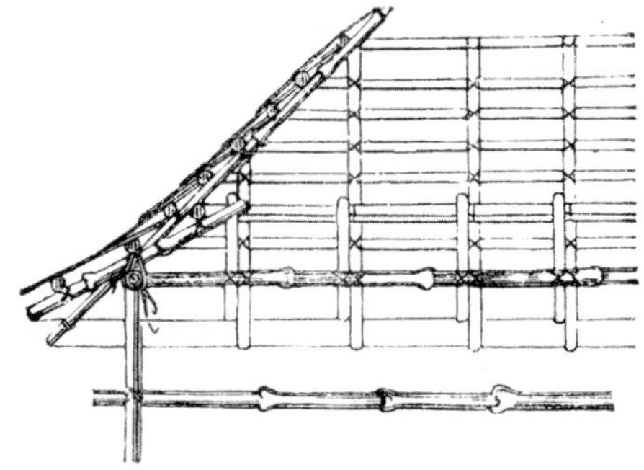

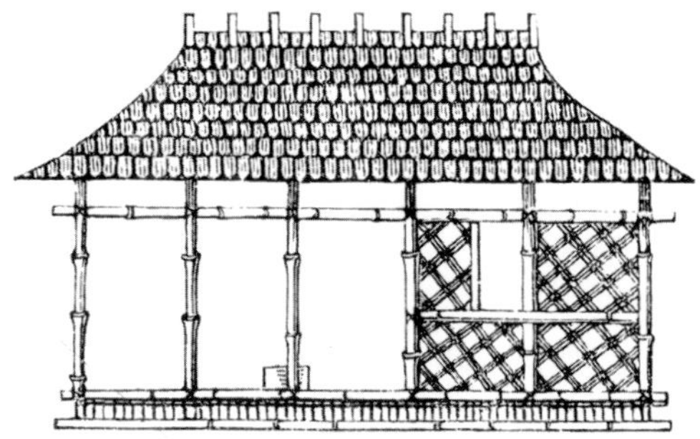

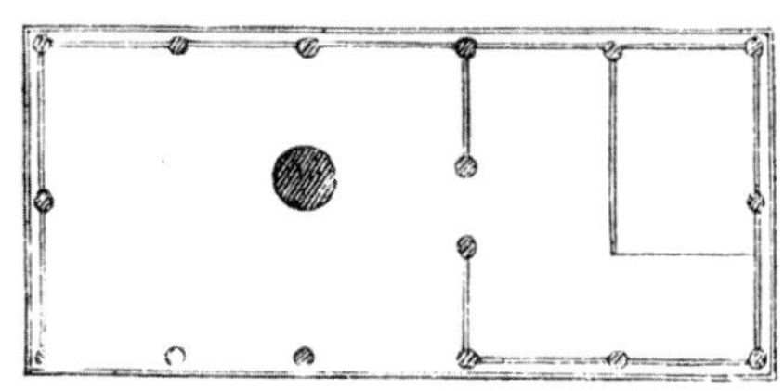

55. Gottfried Semper, floor in the pronaos of the temple of Olympian Zeus, typology of horizontal enclosure with hem and pattern.
56. Gottfried Semper, different types of lace, development of woven surfaces that will become architectural boundary and wall.
57. Gottfried Semper, Caribbean hut, model on display at the Great Exhibition, London, 1851. Architectural enclosure featuring its textile origins.
58. Gottfried Semper, tomb of Midas, textile wall treatment.

union of these two poles; in other words, that the perfectly beautiful form must both express a spiritual content in a characteristic way and present it in a manner pleasing to the eye.«[93]

»When we analyze this concept of architecture, we have the following essential components of a complete building:
1) the covering (that which is suspended),
2) the support (that which stands upright), which at the same time forms the lateral boundary,
3) the substructure, which separates the structure from the natural soil, or the foot (that which lies underneath). Now, these three main parts, which occur in the monuments of all peoples and times are further subdivided into the following absolute architectonic elements (which may be compared with the principal limbs of the animal body) – the interior ceiling, the exterior roof, whose projecting edge forms the cornice, the external walls with doors and windows, the free individual supports (columns and pillars) with their spans, the main foundation and the interior floor. If upper rooms are added above the lower ones, the result is a building with several stories.«[94]

Hübsch defines the essential parts of a building as walls, ceiling, roof, supports, windows, and doors – their specific articulation depending on the material used. He also includes thoughts about the tectonic makeup of a building, defining the »technostatic experience«[95] as related to the structural principles. The discussion that arose around the question of style determined the strong influence that materials and construction methods have had on architectural articulation.

In 1834, Gottfried Semper (1803–1879) published »Vorläufige Bemerkungen über bemalte Architektur und Plastik bei den Alten« (Preliminary remarks about painted architecture and sculpture among the ancients), an essay that differs from Hittorff's thesis only in the way it interprets the background colors. In this paper there is already a suggestion of the theory of cladding that was further elaborated in his aforementioned work *Der Stil in den tektonischen Künsten oder Praktische Ästhetik* (Style in the Tectonic Arts or Practical Aesthetics). He describes the need for layers of paint as simultaneously protective and explanatory. »Wood, iron, and all metals require protective layers to protect them from the corrosive effect of the air«, he writes. »It is quite natural that this requirement is met in a way that at the same time contributes to making them more beautiful. Instead of monotonous whitewash, a variety of pleasing colors are chosen. Polychromy becomes natural, necessary.«[96] In another publication he writes, »It is quite impossible to think and conceive an architectonic work in its true sense without its correct complement of colors; the essence of the forms is dictated by the colors.«[97] Semper evolves the technological need of the newly identified polychromy among the Greeks as something they enjoyed as a means of re-iterating the vivid color combinations they observed in nature. They took advantage of the protective properties of a coating, which allowed wood, clay, and stone to last longer while displaying vivid

59. Otto Wagner, Karlsplatz Stadtbahn station, Vienna, 1899. Façade showing panels with ornamental patterns.
60. Otto Wagner, Karlsplatz Stadtbahn station, Vienna. Corner detail of cladding and metal structure.
61. Otto Wagner, Postsparkasse, Vienna, 1903. Façade with stone cladding. Patterns created by location of metal rivets.
62. Otto Wagner, Postsparkasse, Vienna. Stone cladding on exterior façade seen from the side expressing its a-tectonic nature.

colors.[98] Semper's »Theory of Clothing« states that an understanding of architecture's origin is to be found in the textile realm and that formal language and detailing are based on textile methods of creating a fabric or seams. He describes historic spatial divisions as a carpet draped over poles. With this concept, Semper supports the notion of an architectural skeleton with a skin draped over it, a skin that has turned from textile into brick, stone, or glass. The skin also assumes the role of communication, reflecting the character of the building and still relating to its textile origins through its details. Semper relates his considerations for style closely to the tectonic arts, as he calls them – classifying broad realms of materials and crafts as the sources for stylistic expression. Semper further develops a set of guidelines intrinsic to the notion of textile envelopes: »In this way, justice is done to symmetry or to the correct relation of particular appearance to general, but it is also essential that the general design of the surface clearly indicate that it is either standing upright or hanging. Both cases – namely the surface as a standing wall or as a curtain – are as a rule seen as upright because each is taller than it is wide.«[99] According to Semper's understanding, the architectonic space is divided into walls and wall surfaces and floor dressings with a top cover as »horizontal spatial termination above«.[100] As the concept of religion developed, ornamentation was an important element of the temples of the gods. »Brightly colored distemper«[101] turned into regular forms, contours that stand out, and colored reliefs. »The next step was probably the attempt to imitate the lines of light and shadow observed in such mezzo-relievos by creating color illusions on a flat surface. This is how the first painted forms that encompassed shadow and light came about.«[102] Semper claims. »The vivid colors of textiles explain the polychromy of the wall constructions of antiquity: the German words for wall (Wand) and garment (Gewand) are also etymologically related«,[103] he concludes. Sem- per looks for the typological origin of paint being used to coat ancient temples and develops his »Theory of Clothing« from his observations. The division of architecture into strata is linked to the artisanal origin of all shelter – having its roots in the use of textiles. Architecture consists of »structure, determined by function, and an aesthetic shell«,[104] which is laid over the supporting structure as it gives the building its value and its characteristic features. »These frameworks, which serve to hold, secure, and carry these spatial boundaries, are requirements that have nothing directly to do with space or dividing space. They are alien to the original architectonic idea and initially are not elements that define the forms«,[105] Semper writes. Hans Prinzhorn discusses Semper's »Theory of Clothing«: »The prototype of the wall is the mat hung to act as a spatial border, the rug. Later people begin to construct stone buildings: it turns out that the rug or tapestry is retained to cover the wall, which in itself only has the constructional function of supporting the roof. The rug or tapestry still acts as a spatial boundary. Then someone has the idea of covering the wall with costly stone slabs or metal sheets, or with painted stucco, with wood, terracotta, and so forth: all these types of

cladding, according to Semper, are modifications of that type of spatial border, the mat, the rug«.[106] The Viennese architect Otto Wagner is often said to have executed Semper's theories by showing building skins and their fasteners, communicating the separation of the outer skin from the rest of the building.

Wilfried Wang contrasts Wagner's layered approach with the idea of the architectural monolith: »Thus, layers upon layers remain the last constructional syntax of architecture: the greatest simplicity resides in the panel-like treatment of surfaces. This is essence implied and thus projected, clarity of image and purity of form by default. The compensatory and desperate belief in architecture's semantic radiance was of necessity simultaneous to this gradual process in phenomenal reduction of architecture's real gestation and presence. But rather than consciously redefining Wagner's prediction for contemporary solutions, the underlying nostalgia for a consistent, systematic linear logic, wherein each component of a building is to reverberate in harmony with an originating concept, should be openly discussed in order to avoid a futile effort at redefinition. While such a nostalgia for consistency is undeniably present in much architectural thinking, it is necessary to recall that, just as contemporary constructional technology undermines such a longing for conceptual integrity, so too are formal desires for compact shapes contradicted not only by prevalent detailing standards, but also by the theoretical roots on which the desire for the monolithic architecture has been based.«[107]

Another Viennese architect exploring the a-tectonic articulation of an independent skin is Josef Hoffmann. His Palais Stoclet incorporates the reality of cladding in offering elements that follow the contour of the surfaces and planes, both horizontally and vertically. The marble cladding, spanning the volume with bronze seams at all corners, defies gravity as well as masonry traditions. Although the section of the separation of skin and structure is not revealed, the formal lan-

guage negates gravity and the tectonic rules of a masonry wall. The early 20th century offers numerous examples of architecture wrapped in skins that complement the structure. According to Mirko Zardini, director of the Canadian Centre for Architecture, »Even in the case of a simple building, a small volume, a little box, the skin turns out to be independent, even from the structural viewpoint, from the contents of the building. The facing becomes an element of expression in itself, through the materials used.«[108]

Members of the Dutch De Stijl movement created spatial configurations using layers of painted geometric shapes. The previous all-enclosing thick wall was replaced by paint colors with no thickness at all. 20th-century versions of architectural layering are to be found in architectonic cladding, the separation of skin and skeleton, which advanced through Modernism and resulted in the groundbreaking technology of the curtain wall. Independence from structural requirements offers the designer of the building's skin freedom in terms of materials, formal articulation, and implementation. Cladding can follow the defined volume and remain firmly attached or can act as a partial outer or inner lining, in some instances covering only parts of the spatial enclosure outlining spaces within interiors. Depending on the material, cladding can take the form of a coat of paint or plaster, the thinnest type of sheathing, and in thicker forms can act as planes for paneling or wainscoting.[109] Mark Wigley writes about the use and significance of white paint during the height of Modernism: »What has to be concealed is the fact that the white is a layer. After all, the stripping off of old clothes, advertised by the original promoters of modern architecture and its contemporary dealers, is not simply a stripping of all clothing.«[110]

The collage – from painting to architecture

Gerhard Auer writes, »Most recently in Cubism, Futurism, and constructivism, in collage and decollage, whose synaesthetic methods used the same layering of surface to create a multiperspective without a vantage point.«[111] The architect and writer Richard Weston also connects the term layering to the compositional strategy of Cubism. He describes how »the plans of Le Corbusier's houses of the 1920s can be seen as collage like« and states that Alvar Aalto's Villa Mairea uses multiple layers in a collage-like fashion. He further discusses Colin Rowe and Fred Koetter's *Collage City* publication as accepting a »palimpsest-like layering of time«.[112] Beyond a reference to Carlo Scarpa's interventions in which he adds layers to existing context, Weston cites Tschumi's Deconstructivism as an expression of layering as a formal strategy.[113]

Neoplasticism and other Avant-Garde experiments from the beginning of the 20th century show compositional balance studies with ambiguous layered assemblies. While the architects in early-20th-century Vienna worked on the independent multi-layered wall, the Dutch De Stijl group used layers of paint in two- and three-dimensional studies leading to spatial arrangements. The Cubists explored the outcome of layered sheets of paper and found objects, mechanisms used by painters that would soon translate into architecture and become part of a discussion about transparency and space.

In a master's thesis at the Massachusetts Institute of Technology (MIT), Basel Kotob examines the term spatial layering and discusses the »effect of Cubist concepts on 20th-century architecture and the manifestations of layering in Cubism and their translation from painting into architecture«.[114] Spatial layering starts in the realm of the collage – an arrangement of materials formulating specific compositions from elements with different origins and meanings. Kotob explains further: »The aspect of collage that I believe is critical to this development of the concept of layering in Cubism is the introduction of ›real‹ space. There exists a real space, ambiguous as it may be, that separates the various planes from each other. Cubist collages were closer to architecture than their paintings were as the technique used in ›building‹ then corresponded to some construction methods in architecture. This resulted in the picture becoming architectural, which allowed architects to relate more closely to it.«[115]

This representation of space in Cubist paintings has fascinated theorists and architects. The collage does introduce space into painting, even if it is in micro layers, and it also makes the simultaneous communication of different objects and materials and their content its main focus. The density created by an assemblage is similar to the effect that material layering might create in architecture. Revealing the overlaying elements and related messages or performance is key; depending on how much space is housed between the layers, spatial or material layering is generated.

In a discussion of the art of assemblage, William C. Seitz writes, »In looking backward at the early masterpieces of Cubism one is struck almost as sharply by their connection with the past

63. Vilmos Huszár, Gerrit Rietveld, model for exhibition space, 1924. Layers of colors used to articulate complex spatial configurations.
64. George Braque, *Statue of Horror*, 1913. Collage with overlapping two-dimensional elements.

as by their Modernism. Judged not only by more recent innovations and by the pace of other events that occurred while they were being painted, but also by the 19th-century substratum of Rationalism that preceded them, they seem conservative rather than radical by now. The compression of form and space toward two dimensionality was already implicit in Ingres' *Odalisques*, and an emphasis on juxtaposition was clearly apparent by 1865 in the paintings of Whistler and Manet.«[116] Layered systems were definitely emerging as part of the early-20th-century experiments of abstraction, moving between two and three dimensions but frequently using graphic systems as the basis of architectural concepts. The discussion of transparency acted in that same space between dimensions.

The role of transparency

More recent theoretical links to the evolution of layering can be found in discussions of transparency. The position of layers and their placement in relationship to one another determines their role in a drawing or painting. If two-dimensional planes share the same size and position, their material qualities become visible only at the edges or in cross sections. The partial overlapping of elements makes it possible to experience what lies underneath. The painter and theorist György Kepes investigates the simultaneity of overlapping geometric forms and the resulting spatial effect; with this, he paves the way for a discussion of transparency and space:

»If one spatial form obstructs our view of another form, we do not assume that the second ceases to exist because it is hidden. We recognize, as we look at such overlapping figures, that the first or uppermost has two spatial meanings – itself and beneath itself. The figure, which intercepts the visible surface of another figure is perceived as nearer. We experience spatial differences of depth. Representation of overlapping indicates depth. It creates a sense of space. Each figure appears parallel with the picture-plane and tends to establish a receding spatial relationship.«[117]

Kepes goes on to discuss transparency and superposition:

»Transparency, interpenetration: If one sees two or more figures partly overlapping one another, and each of them claims for itself the common overlapped part, then one is confronted with a contradiction of spatial dimensions. To resolve this contradiction, one must assume the presence of a new optical quality. The figures are endowed with transparency; that is, they are able to interpenetrate without an optical destruction of each other. Transparency however implies more than an optical characteristic; it implies a broader spatial order. Transparency means a simultaneous perception of different spatial locations. Space not only recedes but also fluctuates in a continuous activity. The position of the transparent figures has equivocal meaning as one sees each figure now as the closer, now as the further one. «[118]

In this way, Kepes addresses spatial information that is defined by physical elements perceived simultaneously (while located in different positions); overlapping one another, they maintain their complete form and attributes. Layering in architecture creates this »broader spatial order«[119] described by Kepes, with layering used to reveal a spatial or material sequence. The author and psychologist Rudolf Arnheim describes the overlapping that occurs when one part partially conceals another. The resulting overlap intensifies the relationships between forms, simultaneously comprising the complete form and the fusion. It distracts from the completeness of at least one of the forms involved, and generally all of them. The outcome is not only a correlation – that is, an exchange of energies between independent, completely intact entities. The entities go together, and there is a bond because they reciprocally modify one another.[120] A layered system is perceived at the points of transition from one layer to the next, at the joints and overlaps.

Colin Rowe and Robert Slutzky continue the examination of the concept of transparency within and beyond Cubism. They characterize contemporary architecture of their time, working with superimposition and simultaneity, interpenetration, and ambivalence. While they use Cubist paintings by Picasso and Braque to demonstrate both orders of transparency, they use the term layering in the context of a spatial analysis of Le Corbusier's Palace of the League of Nations.[121] By way of analyzing the »system of spatial layering«,[122] they show a relationship between Le Corbusier's façade of the Villa Garches and Fernand Leger's painting *Three Faces*. The façade consists of fragmentary planes; it is put together »with these parallel planes as a connected whole [...] and the effect of all of them is a vertical stratification of the building's interior«.[123] In the Bauhaus complex, too, they observe spatial layering »presented as a composition of slab-like buildings whose forms suggest the possibility of construing space in layers«.[124] At Garches, Rowe and Slutzky point out the ambiguity in the framing of the window possibly passing behind the wall surface.

While materials can take on the quality of transparency as the ability to be seen through, paintings and architecture, according to Kepes, and Rowe and Slutzky, can be defined by phenomenal transparency, in which superimposed, ambivalent spaces exist through partial overlaps of the planes that demarcate those same spaces. The quality of transparency is expanded in a second essay, in which the authors remove the exclusive relationship of transparency with Cubism and discuss Mile High Center in Denver by I. M. Pei and associates, together with the Farnese Villa at Caprarola, as exhibiting phenomenal transparency. As Slutzky and Rowe state, »Now if Caprarola as well as Denver shows phenomenal transparency, we are obliged to conclude that, after all, it is neither a new of even post-Cubist manifestation.«[125]

65. Clifford Eitel (student of György Kepes), study of transparency, 1944.
66. Colin Rowe and Robert Slutzky, transparency analysis: Palace of the League of Nations.
67. Colin Rowe and Robert Slutzky, transparency analysis: Le Corbusier's villa in Garches.
68. Colin Rowe and Robert Slutzky, transparency analysis: Le Corbusier's still life.

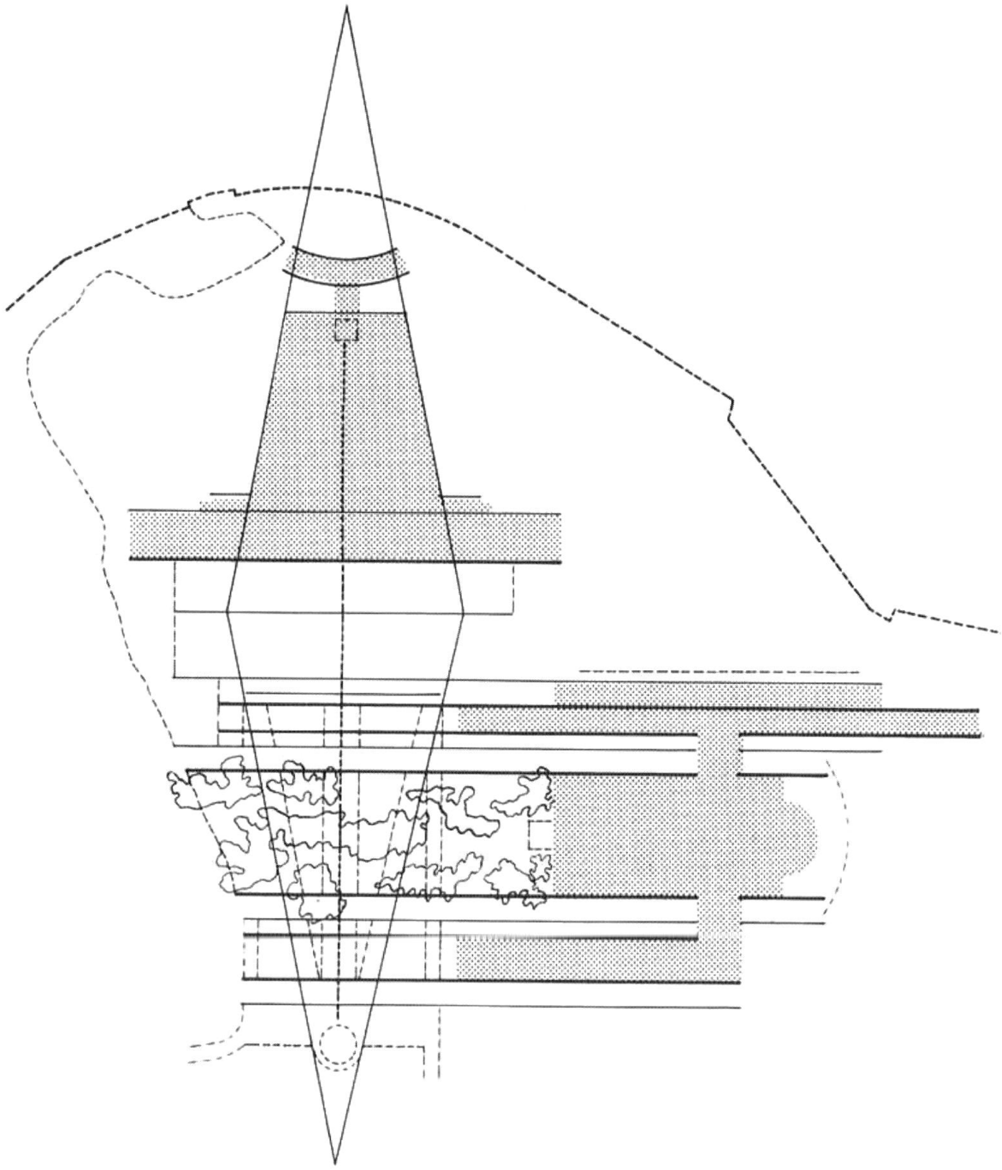

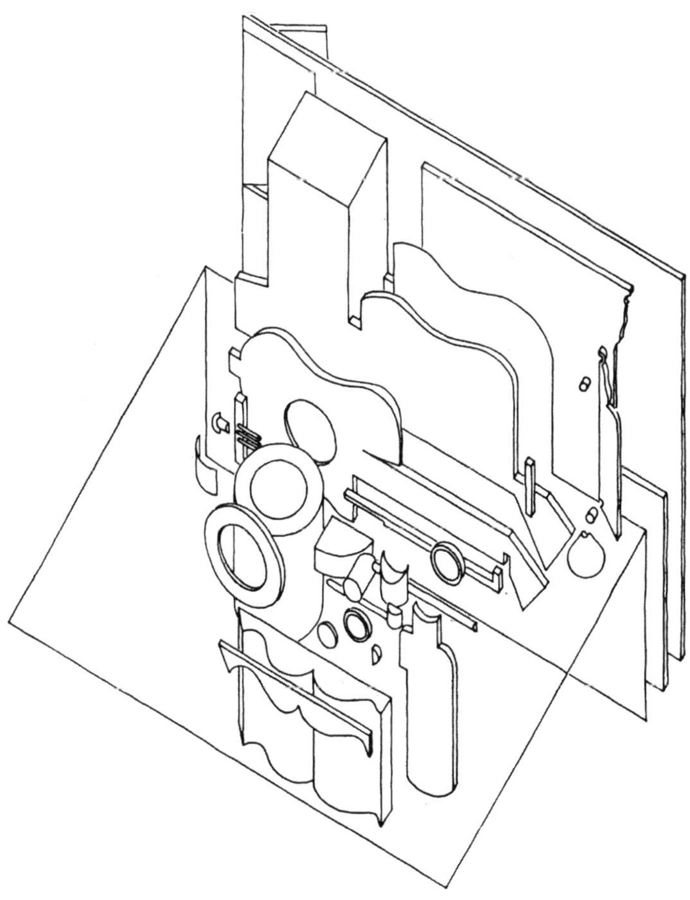

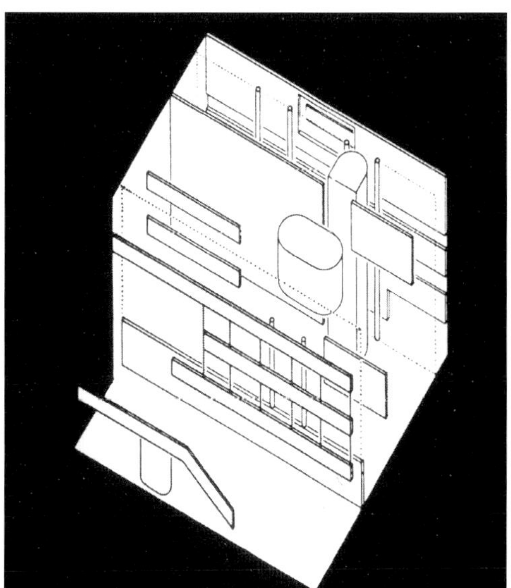

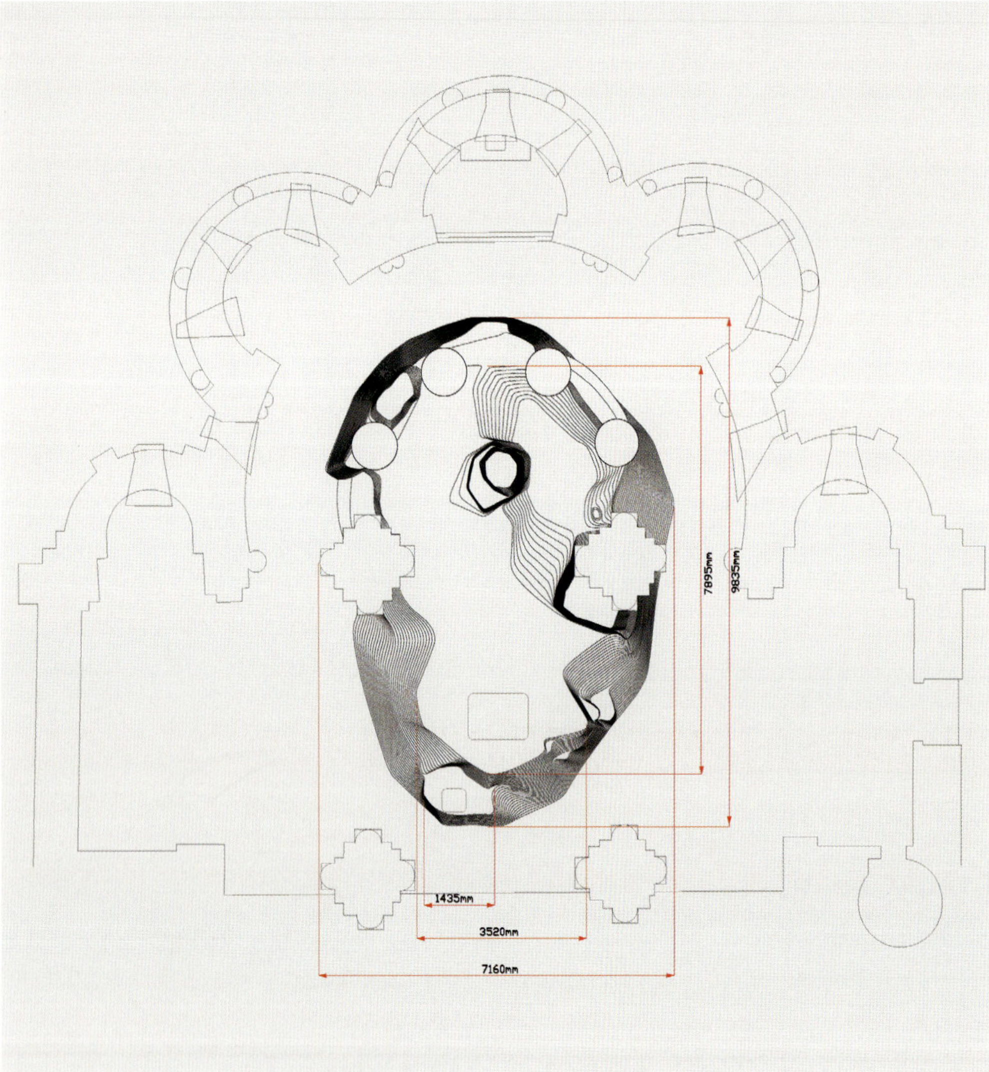

New technology and architectural production – contemporary approaches

More recently, processes based on CNC routers and laser cutters linked to CAD data have demonstrated the potential to generate shapes of dynamic geometries with slight alterations and no need to standardize sizes or dimensions. Using these new methods, an inhabited section or space can be formed by a large quantity of sheets or segments. Multiple surfaces seen in section are frequently used, especially in interiors, expressing depth and uninterrupted continuity and producing all layers at once as a formal move. These multiple segments can evoke a landscape or topography, and the collaged flat layer can be turned perpendicular to become sculptural while still allowing concealment and reprogramming of existing spaces. A multitude of overlaid or slightly spaced sheets lend themselves to carved-out organic spatial contours, suggesting depth and complexity in the form of additional spatial boundaries. The artist Mathieu Lehanneur integrated a new topography into the choir floor of the Romanesque St. Hilaire Church in Melle in western France in 2011. The layered planes recall the sedimented geology of the church's site. The choir furniture is made from Alabaster positioned on the new layers. The topography itself forms baptisterial fountain and vessels for water. The Banq restaurant in Boston, realized in 2008 by Office dA, appears to suspend the multiple layers from the ceiling. Wooden slats clad the columns and ceiling plane, as well as HVAC equipment and generate an organic interior contour of the space while leaving the building's shell unchanged. The layers describe a hanging landscape that is created out of a light abstracted version of topographic layers.

69. Mathieu Lehanneur, choir of St. Hilaire, Melle, France, 2011. New pavement topography embedded as marble layers in the Romanesque church. Plan view.
70. Mathieu Lehanneur, choir of St. Hilaire, Melle, France. New topography embedded as marble layers in the Romanesque church. View from choir into the nave.
71. Mathieu Lehanneur, choir of St. Hilaire, Melle, France. New topography embedded as marble layers in the Romanesque church. View of new layers from above.
72. Mathieu Lehanneur, choir of St. Hilaire, Melle, France. New topography embedded as marble layers in the Romanesque church. View of new layers and existing historic interior.

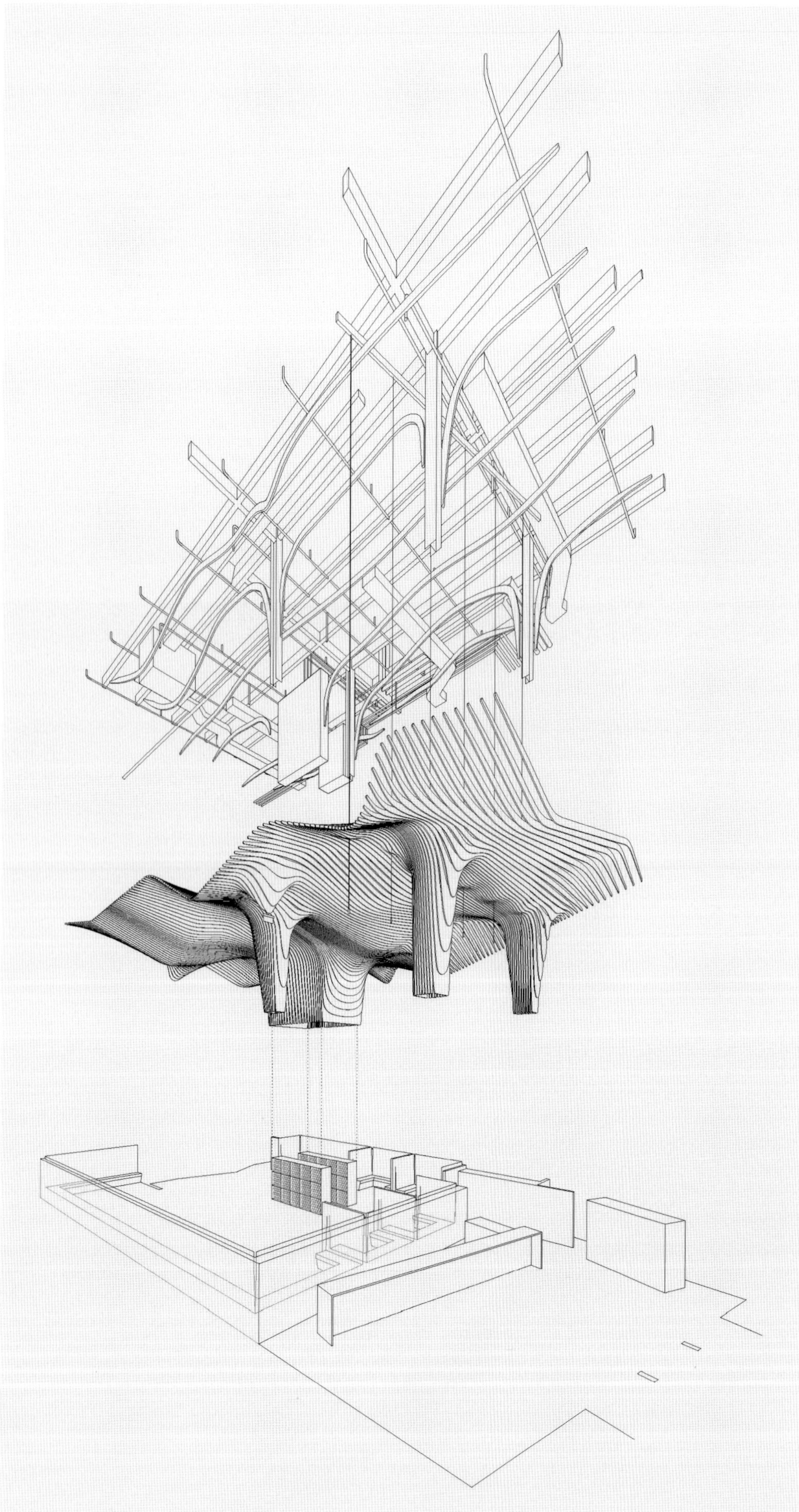

73. Office dA, Banq Restaurant, Boston, 2008. Axonometric drawing.
74. Office dA, Banq Restaurant, Boston. View of the spaced wood slats in the interior of the restaurant cladding ceiling and columns, creating an organically shaped interior.

According to the explorations described above, layering is part of the makeup of the world; peeled-up topographic layers, stacked volumes, and layered façades can all be part of an understanding of architecture as process rather than as a single object of a specific moment. Layering as a compositional principle can be applied in order to expand existing spaces, organize a program, create a hierarchy, or make a formal statement. Typically, these effects are accomplished through a repetitive arrangement of planes, possibly supported by light or water. Layers transporting meaning and perception remain difficult to identify and decode but complement the physical system of the built environment with subjective elements. Layers need to be seen and exposed in section or as an elevation of the strata that exist. The parallel existence offers depth that replaces the strength of a monolith with the complexity of time and humanity. In the following pages, temporal, spatial, and material layering and their functional and formal outcomes are illustrated through examples. It will become clear that the separation of the topic into three distinct types of layers is undermined by several of the phenomena occurring at once in buildings. The material layering that is pulled farther apart to allow a vented façade that also might be inhabitable becomes an example of spatial layering; further elements being added at a later point in time comprise the temporal part of the phenomena. Many more examples could be included; however, the selections presented below serve an illustrative purpose without any claim to comprehensiveness.

Temporal layering: building in historic context

Layering as an architectural tool has been successfully applied in projects involving additions to or alterations of historic structures. Cities with large amounts of historic fabric frequently have adopted or simply evolved along the lines of layering to allow the updating and maintenance of the urban fabric involving the city's infrastructure and its buildings. The entire field of archaeology examines the analysis and identification of multiple layers of civilization deposited over the course of sometimes millennia of changing rulers and related changes in texture and building stock. Updates in available technology, expansions, and shifting formal preferences also lead to continuous changes in the urban fabric. This simultaneous presence of a number of physical updates embeds a social and cultural narrative of cities in their buildings.

Similar mechanisms apply to the continuous updating of buildings accommodating changes not only of program but also of formal and technological characteristics that account for the passing of time. Although the sedimentary nature of layering might seem to be part of the nature of architectural production of any scale, a few 20th-century charters conceptually support a conscious effort to maintain a continuous built narrative.

The 1931 Charter of Athens issued as the outcome of the IV. Congress for Modern Architecture recommended that »fine architecture, whether individual buildings or groups of buildings, should be protected from demolition«, suggesting the value of preservation of notable structures within an evolving urban context. The charter also outlines the importance of avoiding the »re-use of past styles for building new structures« and points to the disastrous consequences of such an approach. The document advocates for the continuing expression of contemporary formal preferences and current technologies leading to an urban palimpsest. Later, in 1966, the Charter of Venice recommended the evaluation of »superimposed work of different periods« and »the revealing of the underlying state« in situations where the removed layer is of little interest while what is uncovered is of great historical value. This charter suggests the analysis and curation of temporal layering in the realm of historic preservation, thus making layering an important part of the design process.

At the scale of the city, temporal layering is created by the insertion of new infrastructure or updated building types. Architecture itself is subject to the changes caused by re-use, alteration, and expansion. The simultaneous presence of new and old in buildings is geometrically achieved by overlapping volumes, planes, or details. Joints and partial overlaps allow visible co-existence and communicate the applied changes. New layers can be wrapped around, inserted, and woven into existing buildings and spaces. Interiors can be newly lined with updated surfaces and equipment. Historically, building material was expensive to acquire and difficult to transport, and ruins frequently were used as quarries. Changes in political power and religious affiliation also impacted the formal organization and formal expression of cities and buildings. Spoils (building parts taken from buildings) symbolize victory and were often integrated into newer buildings.

A growing interest in resourceful construction brings attention to the mechanisms of temporal layering (impacting spatial and material layering as well) in the first decades of the 21st century. High performing façades that minimize energy use within the building tend to be made from multiple layers. If adaptive re-use replaces the demolition of buildings in many instances a layered ensemble of rooms and walls is the result all of which create an integrated and continuous architectural narrative.

75. Duomo in Syracuse, Italy. Baroque façade juxtaposed on a building that evolved over many centuries.
76. Duomo in Syracuse, Italy. Interior detail, Doric column and Romanesque interior.
77. Duomo in Syracuse, Italy. Interior view of the nave, juxtaposition of Romanesque and Doric column placement.

Historic examples

The Duomo in Syracuse in Italy represents 2000 years worth of architectural changes. Its oldest part is of Greek origin, a Romansque nave was placed within the Doric temple most likely in the 11th century, while a Baroque façade was added in the 17th Century. All elements co-exist with the different interventions being perceived almost simultaneously.

The ancient Roman Marcellus Theater (inaugurated by Emperor Augustus in the 1st century BCE) that once offered seating for an audience of around 20 000 was converted into a fortress during the middle ages, turned into a residential palazzo and later into an apartment building.

In 1546 Palladio was commissioned to update the city hall (Palazzo della Ragione which would become the Basilica Palladiana) in Vicenza, Italy. He wrapped the existing town hall structure adding a layer cladding the entire structure with a two-story loggia featuring arched openings and a rhythm of Serliana motifs. Having carefully studied ancient Roman ruins, he contributed to shaping the rise of the Renaissance through a rehabilitation project.

The Uffizi in Florence, Italy represent an integrative intervention by Giorgio Vasari starting in 1560. Civic offices, the tribunal and state archives were brought together in one building which was inserted into the existing urban fabric. A façade featuring a repetitive rhythm of pilasters, pedimented windows and a decorative grid organizing it all accompanies the street-like courtyard. The entire complex is a new layer to a multiplicity of existing small buildings that anchor the new offices. Reconstruction after wars at all times must have resulted in layering of new and old, past and present. Hans Döllgast's treatment of the Alte Pinakothek in Munich integrates a new layer of brick into a wall outlining the geometry of the damage, recording the bombing as part of the building's physical make up (reconstruction/repair 1946–57).

78. Andrea Palladio, Basilica Palladiana, Vicenza, Italy, completed in 1614. Retrofit of an existing Gothic structure – Palladio wrapped the entire building in a new layer acting as a continuous loggia.
79. Marcellus Theater, Rome. Façade reflecting conversion from an antique Roman theater to a residential building.
80. Giorgio Vasari, Uffizi, Florence, Italy, begun in 1560. Façade: new building inserted into existing urban fabric.
81. Giorgio Vasari, Uffizi, Florence, Italy. View into the courtyard, part of the Vasari corridor, connecting the Palazzo Vecchio with the Palazzo Pitti.
82. Leo von Klenze, Alte Pinakothek, Munich, Germany, 1826–36. Restoration after WWII bombing by Hans Döllgast, 1946–57 – new layer visualizing damage that was done to the façade.

For »Il Magistero«, a structure on the campus of Urbino University, the Italian architect **Giancarlo de Carlo** weaves complex volumes into the existing fabric, a three-dimensional volumetric blending of old and new. John McKean describes Il Magistero as »part of town; centered on its virtuosic and many-layered fan-shaped auditorium and on an open drum around which staff rooms cluster. There are no corridors but multiple routes and a range of very different, linked roof gardens.«[126] De Carlo's buildings in Urbino are part of a master plan he developed for this small hill town in the 1950s. His masterplan inserted renovations and new structures into the existing fabric.

83. Giancarlo de Carlo, Urbino, Il Magistero, University of Urbino, Italy, 1968–76. Layered introduction of new spaces into the historic fabric.
84. Giancarlo de Carlo, University of Urbino, Italy. Aerial view: layered introduction of new spaces into the historic fabric.
85. Carlo Scarpa, Banca Popolare, Verona, Italy, 1974–78. New façade facing the piazza.

Venetian architect **Carlo Scarpa** is known for layered interventions in historic fabric. In some instances, he articulates his new spaces through distinct planes in existing historic environments.[127] In Scarpa's work, layering represents a non-hierarchical integration of his formal language into the existing historic context in the Veneto region in Italy. His interventions are distinguished from the existing space with precise overlaps or joints. His goal was not all-encompassing conservation but a critical intervention that didactically reinterpreted the existing structures or interiors. By adding vertical or horizontal layers, Scarpa leaves existing surfaces and details visible and encourages the communication between old and new. He separates floor coverings, walls, and ceilings by joints and frequently applies paneling to surfaces, illustrating the box that is broken open and revealing the layer below. Scarpa conducts experiences of altering spaces through new layers in his numerous exhibition designs, which are often presented in historic interiors that require an additional shell to adapt to the character of the painters or sculptors shown. In his intervention in the eclectic Castelvecchio in Verona (1958–64), Scarpa peels off building layers, adds layers, and enhances the existing spatial layering of the Caserma building through the planes he adds on the floor, which continue through the sequence of spaces. His work takes inspiration from intellectual tendencies with a layered thought process at their core, such as the De Stijl movement, and a strong affinity to Japanese architecture. In his work, planes come together as spaces, with materiality and narrative. Having worked in Venice, Scarpa understands the context of the city as continuously present through layers of stone, water, and light. Clearly distinguished architectural layers are omnipresent in Venice, especially along the Grand Canal where representation was desired. Scarpa combines material layering with a cultural narrative that alludes to Venetian topics in interventions. He continues the heritage of the Viennese architects Josef Hoffmann and Otto Wagner, using a type of textile layering in the form of »Bekleidung« (clothing). Scarpa's transformation of the Sala Manlio Capitolo in the Courthouse of Venice consists of wrapping the existing interior in a layer of wood. The wood cladding speaks of the new architectural intervention but also creates zones within the courtroom. Scarpa creates a separate zone for the judges' space, isolating it from the public auditorium, which is supported by a change in floor level. The wood skin is structured by a regular pattern of nails, which add a precise and graphic appearance to the mahogany wood. Scarpa worked in the city of Venice for many years of his career, and therefore the context of the city is continuously present through layers of material, water, and light. In the Querini Stampalia Foundation (1961–63), he overlays the existing surfaces in many instances and with a multiplicity of different planes. He articulates the floors to allow the water of the adjacent canal to rise into the building, emphasizing the Venetian character of the setting. Water and its reflective qualities acts as one of the elements that define new spaces. The Querini Stampalia Foundation has been altered and renovated several times since Scarpa's intervention, continuing the narrative and history of the palace. The façade of Scarpa's Banca Popolare in Verona (1974 to 1980) exhibits a multi-layered façade that ties in with the horizontal cornices of its neighboring buildings. A thick, stepped skin provides a quantity of depth and ample reflection of light and shadow. The fenestration plane of the windows varies in location from floor to floor, a complex thickness that suggests a late-20th-century version of the curtain wall. On the interior, double walls act as light vessels that display depth.

86. Carlo Scarpa, court room Sala Manlio Capitolo, Venice, 1955. Wood paneling along walls of existing court room.
87. Carlo Scarpa, Banca Popolare, Verona, Italy, 1973–80. Interior-wall detail made from a double layer of elements.
88. Palazzo Abatellis, Palermo. 15th century palace, intervention by Carlo Scarpa, 1953/1954. Interior stucco panels creating space for exhibited sculpture.
89. Palazzo Flangini, Canal Grande, Venice. Side view of representative façade layer facing the Grand Canal.
90. Carlo Scarpa, Paul Klee exhibition, Venice, 1948.
91. Carlo Scarpa, Toulouse Lautrec exhibition, Museo Correr, Venice, 1952.
92. Carlo Scarpa, Castelvecchio, Verona, Italy, 1958 to 1964. View into the spatial sequence of Caserma.
93. Carlo Scarpa, Fondazione Querini Stampalia, Venice, 1961–63. Entry area with material layers on floor, wall and ceiling.
94. Carlo Scarpa, Fondazione Querini Stampalia, Venice. Entry gate.

Scarpa's approach to existing context has brought followers, for example, the German architect **Karljosef Schattner**, whose architecture contributes to a dialogue of new and old in the historic city of Eichstätt, Germany. Schattner's projects in Eichstätt, a medieval city with Baroque updates, allowed a new measurement and perception of the existing context, almost as if his structures created an enhanced perception. Schattner expresses his sense of the city as a system that continuously changes: »Failure to make fresh contributions to the town or city, to add to their architectural development, would be disastrous. In the past towns and cities experienced constant change.«[128]

95. Karljosef Schattner, Katholische Universität, School of Journalism, Eichstätt, Germany, 1985 to 1987. Integration of historic and contemporary buildings, detail.
96. Karljosef Schattner, Katholische Universität, School of Journalism, Eichstätt, Germany. Integration of contemporary addition in historic courtyard.
97. Enric Miralles and Benedetta Tagliabue, EMBT, Santa Caterina Market, Barcelona, Spain, 2005. Site plan.

In Spain, **Enric Miralles** and **Benedetta Tagliabue (Miralles/Tagliabue, EMBT)** integrated the historic market of Santa Caterina (2005) in Barcelona into a new building complex, combining the partial restoration and modernization of the structure with a new system in plan covered by a large and colorful undulating roof. In a type of architectural geology, the building is situated atop the foundations of a Dominican convent and a burial crypt, which themselves were built on top of remains from buildings from previous centuries. Miralles and Tagliabue continued the historic superimposition without favoring one era over another, treating the existing walls and parts as objets trouvés, making them part of the site condition and creating a timeless narrative. The intervention is profound and affirmative, allowing the new order to take over the existing parts and profoundly altering the scale of the existing elements, while the large roof unites all of the pieces.

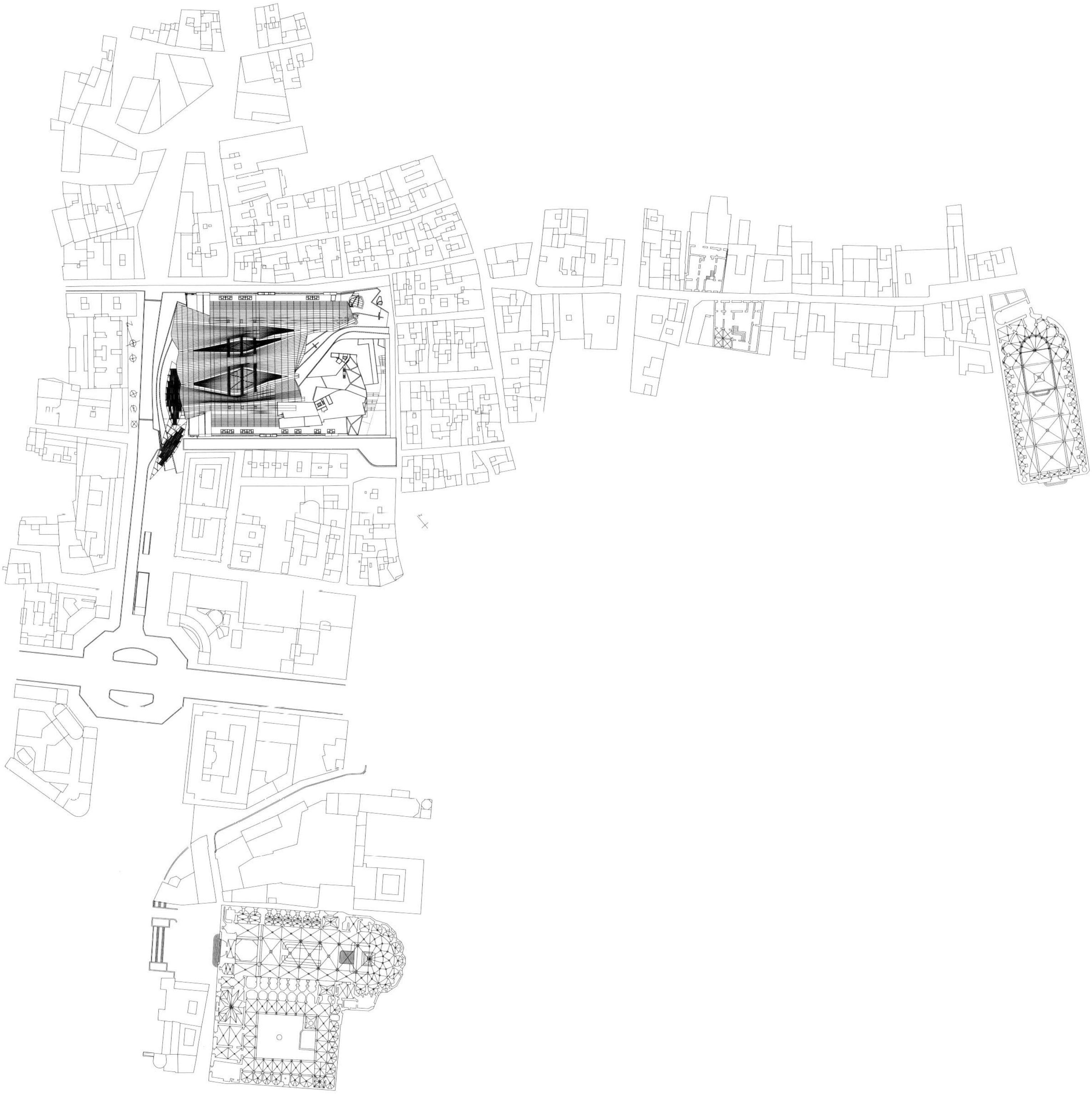

Mark Wigley writes, »Miralles' work was initially generated by working on the plan and by superimposing plans.«[129] Miralles uses his projects to re-define the site – its history and topography. »Time becomes peripheral when you start to work on buildings from another century«, Wigley continues. »They are the outer limits of the present. What happens here is that the layers of time are what you can't identify precisely, and you have to go back and re-define them.«[130] The city hall in the Dutch city of Utrecht adds to a series of civic buildings located at the same place for more 650 years, integrating existing parts with a new wing. The façades of the buildings communicate the growth and fragmentation that accompany a historic continuum. The interior combines the old and the new in a continuous discourse, allowing moments of surprise, evoking memories but also raising questions about the role of architectural fragments and monumentality.

98. Enric Miralles and Benedetta Tagliabue, EMBT, Santa Caterina Market, Barcelona, Spain, 2005. Exterior.
99. Enric Miralles and Benedetta Tagliabue, EMBT, Santa Caterina Market, Barcelona Spain. View of new roof added to existing complex.
100, 101. Enric Miralles and Benedetta Tagliabue, EMBT, Utrecht City Hall, Utrecht, The Netherlands, 2000. Exterior.
102. Enric Miralles and Benedetta Tagliabue, EMBT, Utrecht City Hall, Utrecht, The Netherlands. Site plan.

More recently, **McCullough Mulvin Architects** in Dublin, Ireland, show a layered approach to new buildings and expansions in a historic context, weaving the new into the existing, favoring the clear expression of planes and their edges in the urban exterior and the building's interiors. New volumes are superimposed on a tight urban context, and planes re-define the floor, wall, and ceiling surfaces in the implementation of the new spaces. Raymond Ryan writes about the Waterford City library: »The project – now L-shaped with the addition of the new site – offered opportunities for juxtaposition between a modern building and a layered intervention into the fabric, especially in the manipulation of section and light to create a new diagonal circulation across the plan.«[131] The interior is lined with dark timber, allowing glimpses of the existing structure while completely re-defining the interior. Rush Library is a converted church that balances conservation, interpretation of the existing with the new – walnut planes that reshape the interior of the nave.

Temporary layering uses spatial or material layers to add and expand structures and environments over time, sometimes to adjust program or to gain space, in other instances to adjust to changing stylistic expectations or to adapt to new technologies.

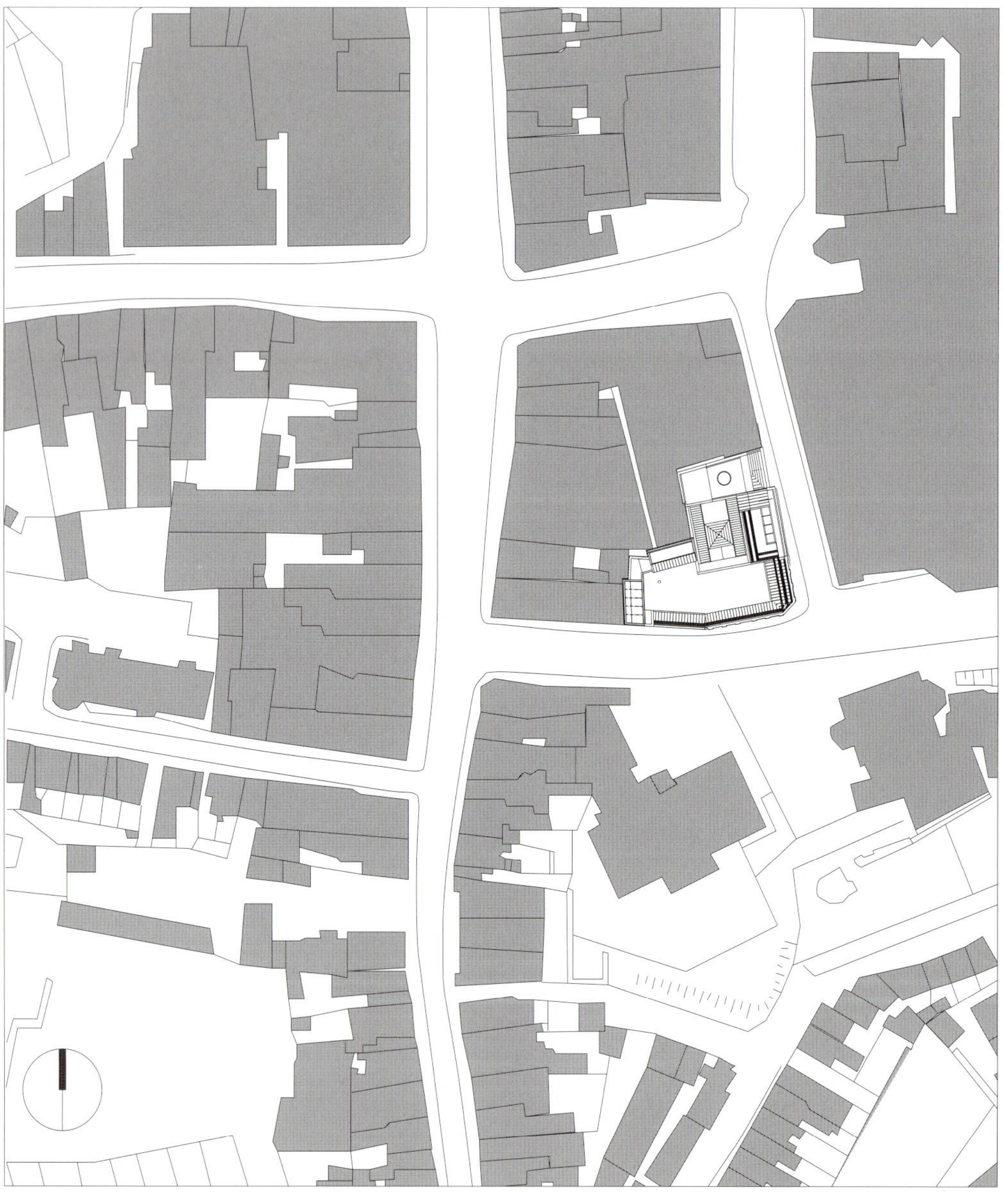

103. McCullough Mulvin Architects, Waterford Library, Waterford, Ireland, 2005. Site plan.
104. McCullough Mulvin Architects, Waterford Library, Waterford, Ireland. Exterior.
105. McCullough Mulvin Architects, Rush Library, Rush, Ireland, 2005. Interior layering of new wooden elements.
106. McCullough Mulvin Architects, Rush Library, Rush, Ireland. Plan.
107, 108. McCullough Mulvin Architects, Rush Library, Rush, Ireland. Interior layering of new and existing elements.

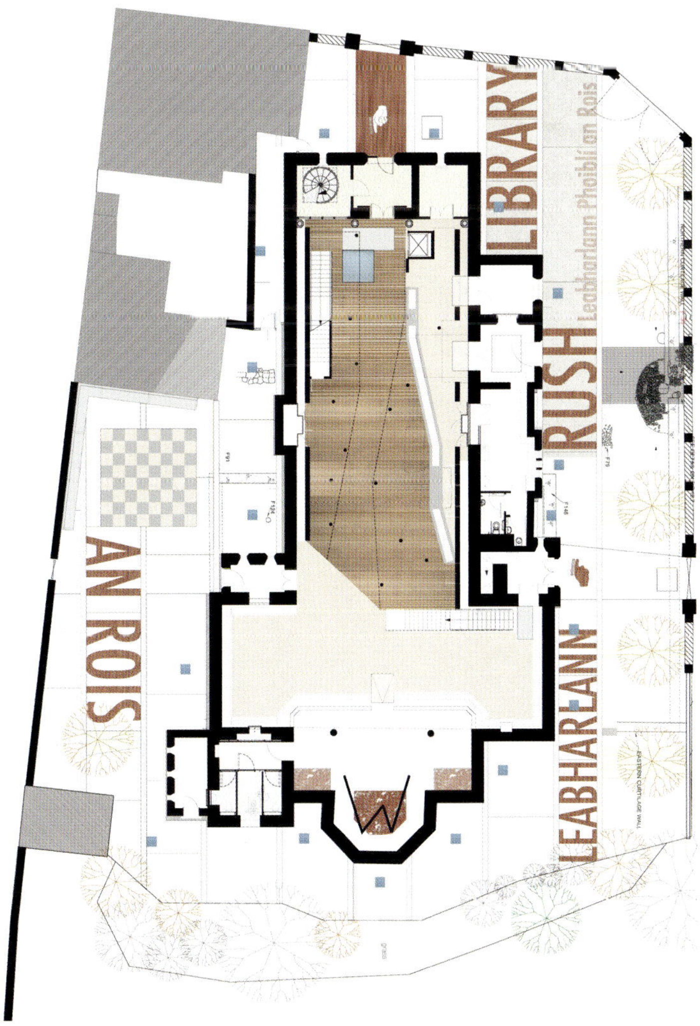

Spatial layering: in-depth sequences of hierarchy and program

Spatial layering in buildings is generated by a sequential arrangement of spaces defined by walls, openings, or various types of enclosures. Time and chronology frequently play an intrinsic role in the distinction of spatial layers, while other spatial sequences might be organized by program or desired atmosphere. Additive arrangements of volume, mass, and skin create complex spatial systems, sometimes working in plan, while at other times being more prevalent in section or elevation. As this exploration concentrates on layering that is revealed and based on an intentional decision – a design and analysis tool – spatial layering requires the sequence to be perceived simultaneously. While predominantly related to physical enclosures, spatial layers are accompanied by functional and cultural information – immaterial components based on perception. Light, water, and color can also enhance or even generate a rhythm of spatial layers. Enlarged thresholds and specifically articulated transition zones may support a hierarchy of spaces, especially in sacred, civic, or entertainment buildings.

Instead of relying on walls, spatial layers can be distinguished solely through changes in materiality or surface treatment that create zones within one larger volume – a phenomenon closely connected to material layering.

European Medieval cities or castles are surrounded by multiple spatial layers for defense, with clear lines of separation created by walls or moats. Sequential expansions visibly express a building's growth over time and tie in once more with a built chronology that unites temporal and spatial layering. In other instances, the formal arrangement of spatial sequences acts as a demonstration of wealth and power used to impress or intimidate outsiders.

Throughout the period of architectural Modernism, spatial layering has supported the free plan and allowed the integration of programmatic and spatial relationships. Especially in the area of housing, the transition from public to private areas often includes a layered approach that spatially supports the functional shifts. The exterior (gardens or views into surrounding landscape) frequently is part of the overall arrangement, leading to a fluid integration of interior and exterior spaces.

The examples below demonstrate how a distinction among the types of layering remains conceptual; the component of time will play a role in many of the examples presented. Some examples, such as those by Peter Eisenman, work with the geometric intricacy of a collage type of arrangement of spaces and planes. Other examples use rhythm and light to support the spatial layering, as evident in Leiviskä's buildings. All of the case studies have in common the simultaneous experience of spaces of different quality and function, taking advantage of a complex sense of temporal, spatial, and functional orientation.

109, 110. Peter Eisenman, study of Giuseppe Terragni's Casa del Fascio, 1932–36. Layering of internal planes.
111. Peter Eisenman, House IV. Axonometric drawing showing spatial layering.
112. Peter Eisenman, Wexner Center for Visual Arts, Ohio State University, Columbus, 1989. Façade, volumes with references to the past, showing elevation of rotated grids.

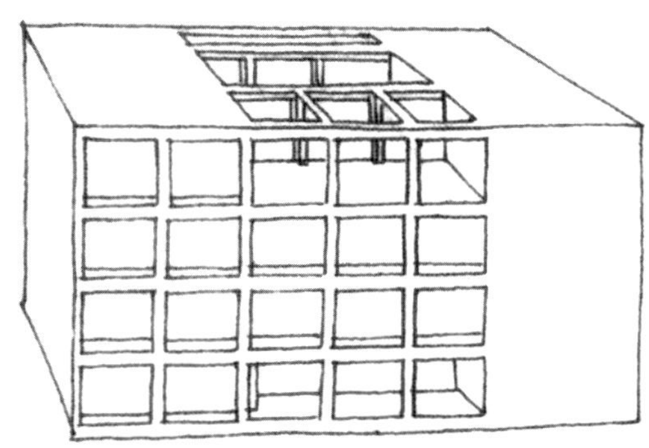

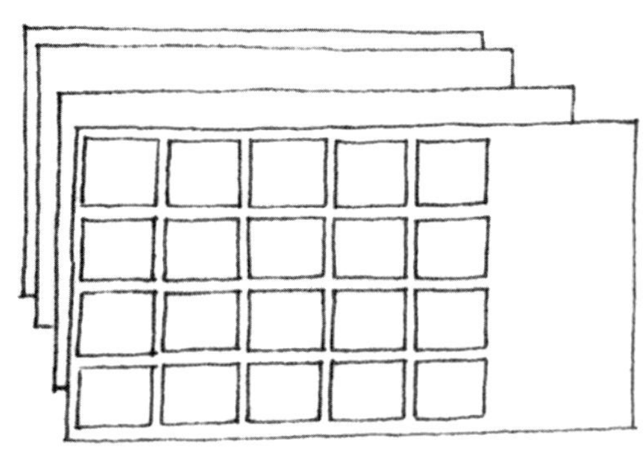

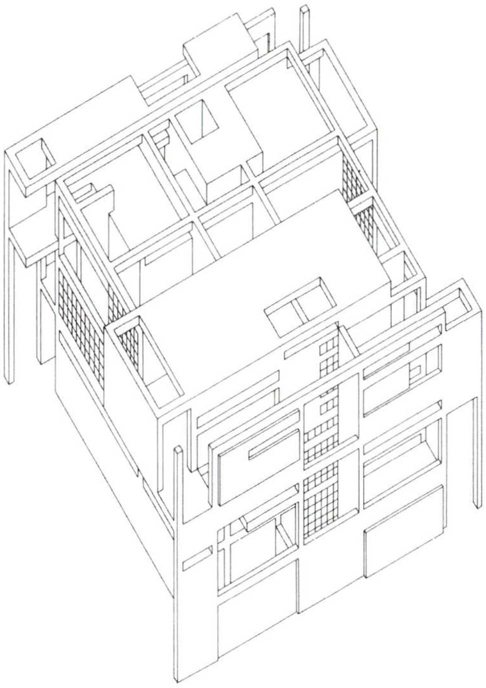

The work of **Peter Eisenman** exemplifies the interplay of various types of layering. In his dissertation on the formal basis of modern architecture, Eisenman examines the dialectic of mass and surface, especially apparent in his analysis of Giuseppe Terragni's work. For Eisenman, mass represents »the generic internal state«,[132] and surface »an internal-external conflict«. He identifies three volumetric systems and their close relationships to the surface, identifying the link between spatial and material layering. Eisenman's early architectural work reflects his research related to mass and surface, excavation and decomposition as a type of inverted layering, leading to complex spatial arrangements in his experimental houses. Aaron Betsky calls the designs a process of »feeding the structures of architecture back into themselves, overlaying, colliding, and extruding multiple ordering principles in order to create complicated layers of possible coherence, all unresolved«.[133] In describing house IV, Eisenman writes that »plan and section is now a series of layers with a distinguishing of a lateral and orthogonal axis«.[134] The layering in Eisenman's houses is prominently featured in the published documentation, in which wall segments are highlighted in axonometric representations of the grid-based volumes. Superimposed grids suggest a layering of zones and create spaces in-between the systems, expressing transitions and the existence of the in-between. In the documentation of his first six houses, Eisenman shows the process of formal (de)composition and the development of volumes and elements out of a fragmentary use of the plans. House II's development and construction principles are described by sketches of wall segments that generate a series of spatial layers and are complemented by three-dimensional grids, which turn a layered composition into a geometrical process involving grids. Eisenman's Wexner Center for Visual Arts, at Ohio State University (1989), displays the encounter of grids at different scales. Eisenman demolishes the existing tower in order to build a substitute tower from the same material, formulating the entrance to the Center for Visual Arts. Layering in this case involves interaction with memory and the simultaneous transformation of the physical and metaphorical past. As Richard Weston analyzes it, the project »was similarly designed by overlaying multiple layers of spatial order. Some were purely formal – the Modernist grid, represented by a steel ›scaffolding‹ ; others site-specific, such as the play on the offset of the campus grid from that of the city, which followed the Jefferson Grid; and others – notably the fragments of a demolished brick ›fortress‹ – were narrative.«[135] Various grids are juxtaposed, which serves to define the site, the building, and the interiors. Although many buildings throughout Eisenman's career might reflect a sense of layered conceptual realities, his project for the City of Culture of Galicia (CCG) in Santiago de Compostela, Spain, completed in 2011 involves the architectural transformation of the site's topography with roof planes and built volumes. The surface of the site becomes walls and roofs, buildings become part of the landscape, and the landscape-streets become voids cut into these lifting layers. Shifting grids are used for structure and skin, leading to another overlay pattern and allowing simultaneous readings of both.

113. Peter Eisenman, CCG, Santiago de Compostela, Spain, 2011. Massing suggesting topographic architectural layers.
114. Peter Eisenman, CCG, Santiago de Compostela, Spain. Topographic architectural approach appearing in façade.
115. Peter Eisenman, CCG, Santiago de Compostela, Spain. View of the roof.
116. Louis Kahn, Exeter Library, Exeter, New Hampshire, 1965–71. Exterior brick skin shown as a separate layer opening up the corner of the building.
117. Louis Kahn, Exeter Library, Exeter, New Hampshire. Interior view of layered elements made from wood and concrete.

Louis Kahn's Exeter Library, completed in 1972, offers a concentric organization of spatial layers with two components of skin pulled apart, making them inhabitable and working around a core of functions related to the library program. With a brick outer shell and a concrete inner shell, usage is differentiated by lighting conditions and materials. Explaining how he separates the wall into interior and exterior layers, Kahn states, »Because a wall has an interior which is different from an exterior [...] we have to come to the point where this realization now can separate an exterior wall from an interior wall New Hamp-shire [...] and create space between them that you could walk between, that which you couldn't do with a solid stone wall.«[136]

Another challenge to the conventional definition of interior and exterior is found in **Juha Leiviskä**'s work, which displays a rhythm of walls that articulate slivers of closed and open spaces. Männistö Church and Parish Center (1992) in particular features a staggering arrangement of walls equivalent of contrasting light and dark in the interiors by layering walls and light. Malcolm Quantrill sees the origins of Leiviskä's work in the layered textures and experiences of Aalto's Modernism as well as the interpenetrating geometries of the De Stijl movement. Quantrill writes, »Aalto's complex layering of volumes and surfaces imbued his architecture with its own very personal being. Perhaps we might, therefore, understand Aalto's achievement as one of the building bridges between abstract, modernist and purist concepts and the more available world of human experience and response. The play of form and material textures in light is fashioned in Aalto's hands by the processes of layering and filtering.«[137]

118. Juha Leiviska, Männistö Church and Parish Center, Kuopio, Finland, 1992. Exterior with layered walls expressed.
119. Juha Leiviska, Männistö Church and Parish Center, Kuopio, Finland. Site plan.
120. Juha Leiviska, Männistö Church and Parish Center, Kuopio, Finland. Interior.

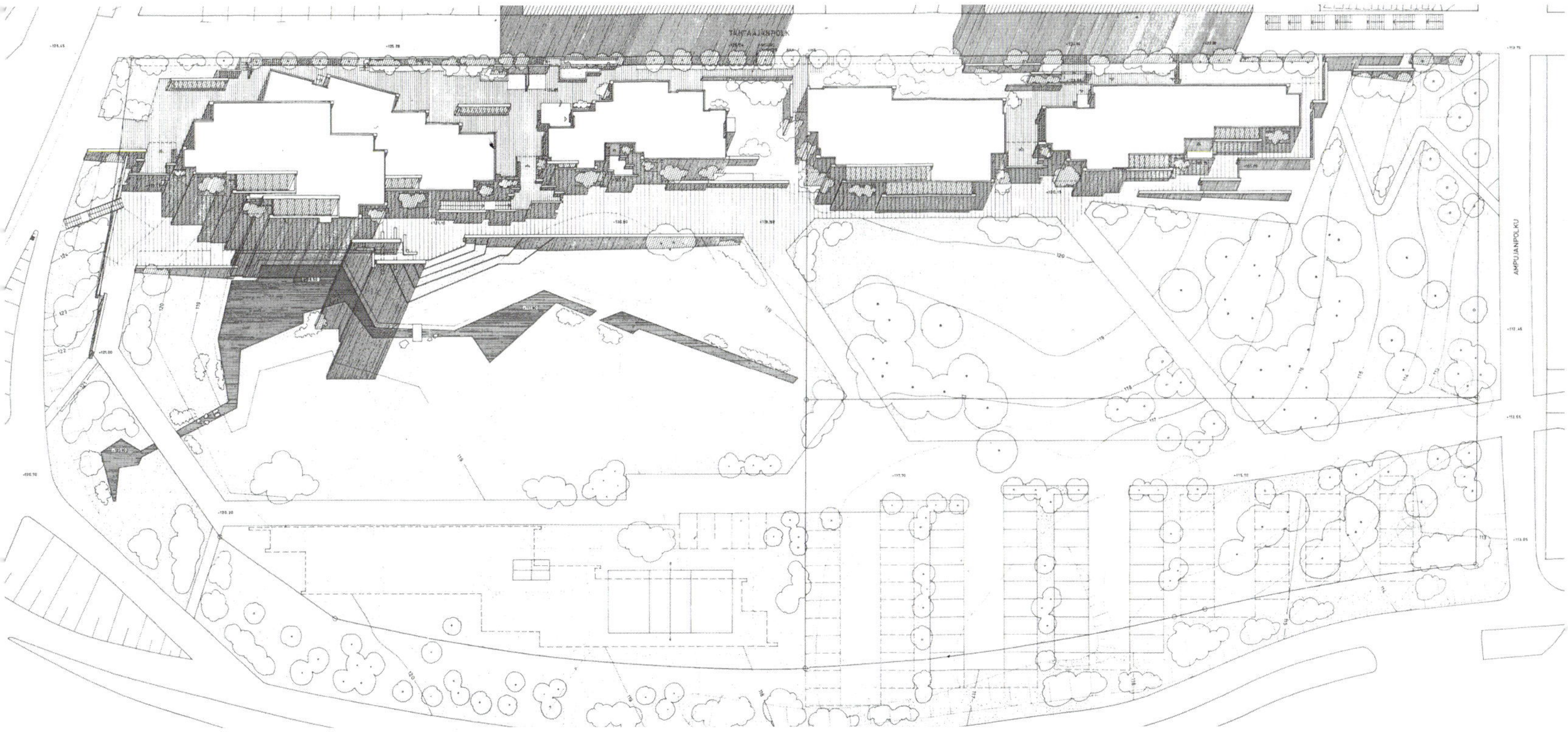

Ram Karmi and **Ada Karmi-Melamede** use spatial layering as an interior and programmatic strategy to create transition, for example, in their building for the Supreme Court in Jerusalem, Israel (1992). The complex is organized along overlaid axes that relate to different parts of the historic and contemporary city. The meeting point of the axes symbolizes the interaction needed between executive, legislative and judicial branches of government and offers a shared public space for all. Separate volumes house a library, the courtrooms, the judges' chambers and a parking garage.

Lighting is used to articulate buffer spaces between key parts of the program. The foyer that leads to the courtrooms is organized in parallel slices of stone, light, and white stucco, with the rough stone surfaces reminiscent of the historic walls of Jerusalem.

121. Ram Karmi and Ada Karmi-Melamede, Supreme Court of Israel, Jerusalem, 1992. Courtyard, spatial layering of mass and void.
122. Ram Karmi and Ada Karmi-Melamede, Supreme Court of Israel, Jerusalem. Foyer, spatial layering of light and materials.
123. Hitoshi Abe, University of Economics and Business, Vienna, Austria, 2013. Student center, interior spatial layers articulated through color.
124. Hitoshi Abe, University of Economics and Business, Vienna, Austria. Student center, exterior.
125. Hitoshi Abe, University of Economics and Business, Vienna, Austria. Student center, axonometric drawing of layering.

Hitoshi Abe completed the student center building for the new campus of the University of Economics and Business in Vienna, Austria, in 2013. In a documentary[138] Abe talks about the layering of activities that is guided by the layered volumes and outdoor spaces. Long skinny masses with ondulating façades on one side overlap each other in irregular spacing creating pedestrian roads and courtyards. The spatial layering continues on the interior articulated by material transitions often especially perceivable in areas of circulation, staircases and hallways. Spatial layering offers a series of non-hierarchical indoor and outdoor spaces as part of a new university campus establishing a collaborative and open environment.

Jürgen Mayer H.'s Mensa Moltke (student dining hall) in Karlsruhe, Germany uses its structural system to generate porous spatial layers he calls elastic spaces. The mono colored porous structure creates a cage like pattern that articulates the different uses within the dining hall.

The mono colored structure creates a cage like pattern that articulates the different uses within the dining hall. The structure represents an irregular space frame that can be associated with the treed surrounding of campus. There is no differentiation between interior and exterior spaces, areas with different programmatic uses can be used separately and offer flexibility. The colonnades don't only form the framework for the façade but also the interior separation articulating a complex system of spatial layers.

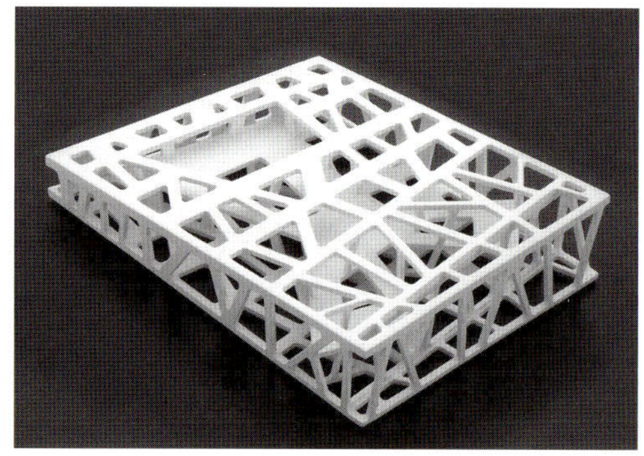

126. Jürgen Mayer H., Mensa Moltke, Karlsruhe University Campus, Karlsruhe, Germany, 2007. Exterior.
127. Jürgen Mayer H., Mensa Moltke, Karlsruhe University Campus, Karlsruhe, Germany. Interior.
128. Jürgen Mayer H., Mensa Moltke, Karlsruhe University Campus, Karlsruhe, Germany. Model.
129. Hascher Jehle Architektur, Kunstmuseum Stuttgart, Stuttgart, Germany, 2005. Façade carrying changing information layers.
130. Ludwig Mies van der Rohe, Kaufhaus C & A Brenninkmeyer, Stuttgart, project, 1928.

Material layering: multiple-skin envelopes

Material layering constitutes spatial layering without voids between individual planes and layers, representing the direct superimposition of elements simultaneously perceived. Material layering can include the expression of architectural planes deposited over time, skins overlapping one another based on desired or necessary changes in exterior or interior walls. Used as a design tool, material layering generates thickness and exhibits depth; it folds, wraps, and sometimes moves building skins. Material layering typically involves façades and their formal, energetic, and narrative performance. Modernism of the early 20th century promoted light, thin, and transparent enclosures to replace traditionally thick masonry walls. Based on the separation of skin and skeleton during the Industrial Revolution, façades became complex arrangements of elements insulating, shading, and defining the interior as part of a larger urban landscape. The glass curtain wall communicates transparency and openness, especially in Post-War Europe, its lightness suggesting a democratic society that is visible through layers of air and glass.

Adding advertisement, information, and interactive projections to a multi-layered curtain wall results in what is commonly called a »media façade«. Starting with simple but well-lit signs that provide information about the company that owns or occupies a building, architects also use a building's skin as an electronic display for static or dynamic information and transform it into a communication tool and interactive system to engage the visitor. Computer screens can be added to a building's exterior, reversing the traditional function of a window and making the structure a mast for the message. Information, text, images, or video can be displayed on a façade with the projection surface integrated into the glazing. Other approaches include moving mechanical parts (kinetic façades) or lights that are controlled by software displaying anything from films and images to merely changing patterns.

The Stuttgart Kunstmuseum by the architects Hascher Jehle presents a transparent glass cube with a stone clad core to the historic downtown. The façade carries a changing layer of information regarding exhibits and events that is projected onto the spaces by the light entering the spaces.

In 1928 Mies van der Rohe proposed a façade for the Stuttgart Bank that united the inhabiting business' signs and the building's curtain wall, embedding a layer of information into the skin. This type of information layer was already discussed in the context of Las Vegas or New York's Times Square, which feature façades that send messages and present advertisement. The media façade presents an expanded version of Mies's project of integrating information technology and interactivity into the architecture.

Contemporary material layering works with the continued evolution of high-performance building skins that conserve or produce energy for the building and allow a precisely regulated room climate. The examples below feature skins that address the climatic conditions within the building by using separate layers and take advantage of the narrative of complexity and responsible sustainability.

Enhanced transparency simultaneously expressing both, spatial layering and material layering is dominant in the German Pavilion of the World Fair in Brussels 1958 by **Sep Ruf** and **Egon Eiermann**. The complex is comprised of a series of eight pavilions based on square plans, connected through covered walkways – all based on a repetitive and standardized grid for structure and fenestration. The façade itself expresses lightness and light. It is set back and offers openings for natural ventilation, while a fine metal structure was installed with generous spacing from the glass, allowing vertical sunshading at the end of the roof overhang. An integrated and minimized system of linear metal elements wraps the low volumes made from concrete slabs.

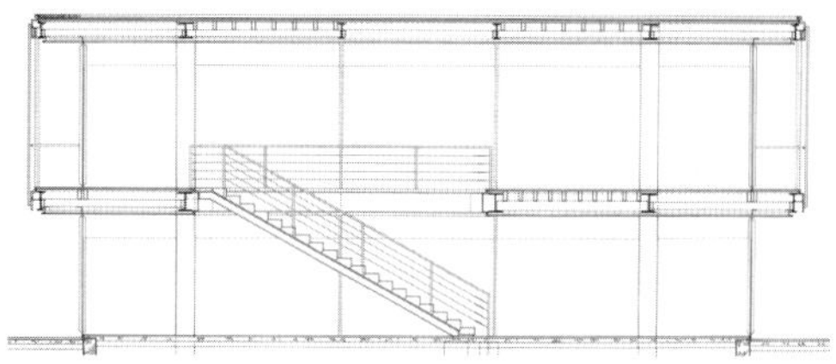

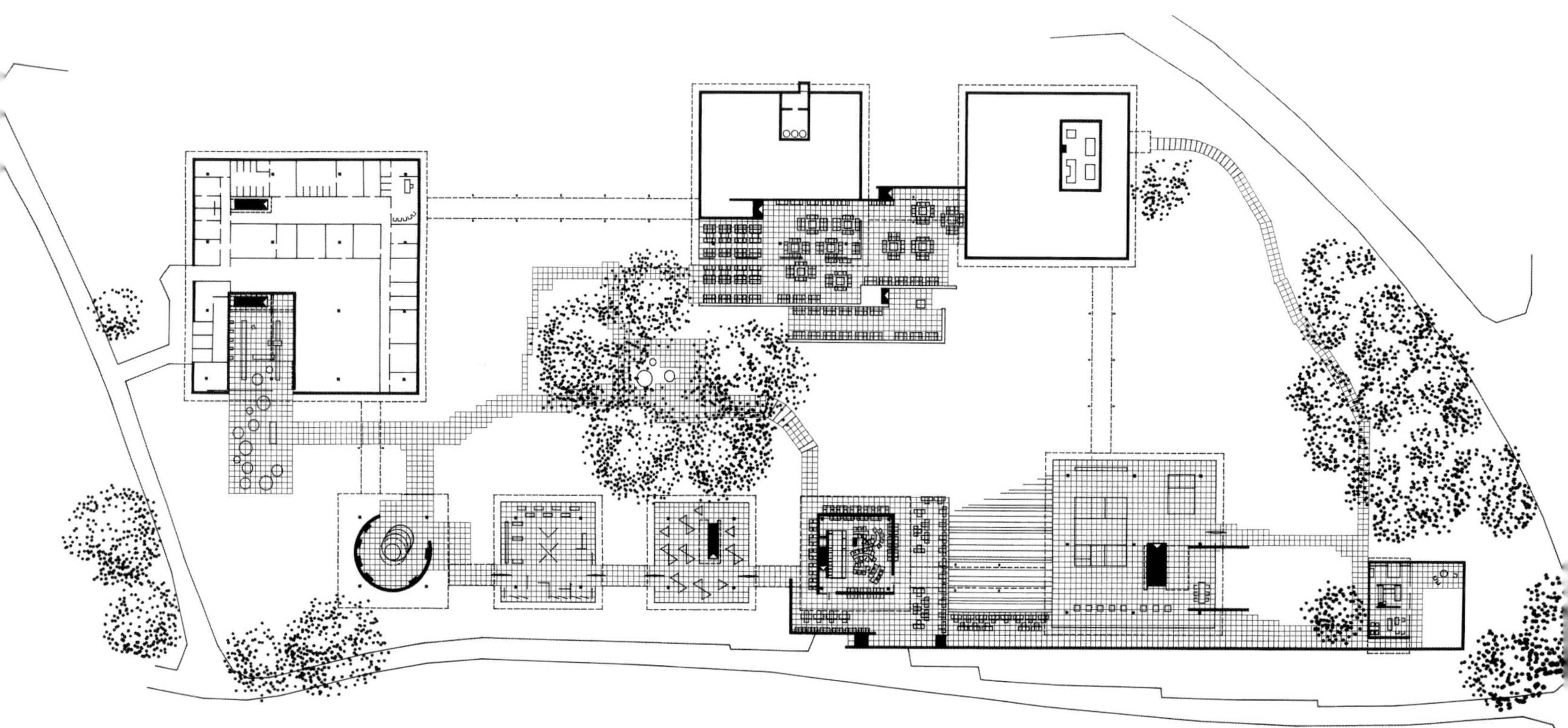

131. Sep Ruf and Egon Eiermann, German Pavilion at Brussels World Fair, Brussels, 1958. General view with double-layered façades, typical for Eiermann.
132. Sep Ruf and Egon Eiermann, German Pavilion at Brussels World Fair, Brussels. Site plan.
133. Sep Ruf and Egon Eiermann, German Pavilion at Brussels World Fair, Brussels. Section.
134. Norman Foster, Sainsbury Centre for Visual Arts, Sainsbury, England, 1978. Façade sketch.
135. Norman Foster, Sainsbury Centre for Visual Arts, Sainsbury, England. Façade.
136. Norman Foster, Sainsbury Centre for Visual Arts, Sainsbury, England. Axonometric drawing of the structure and the layered skin.

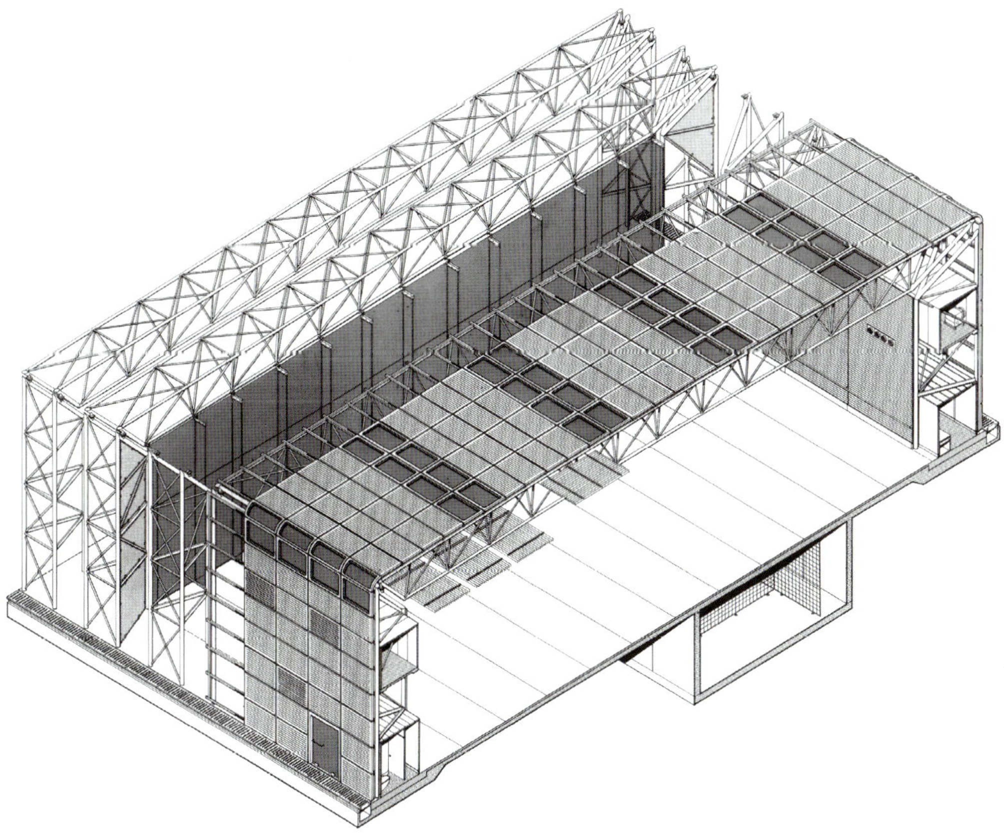

One example of the façade taking on a multitude of functions is **Norman Foster**'s Sainsbury Centre of the University of East Anglia, completed in 1978. This building exhibits the beginning of a long research endeavor for multiple-layered skins. In the project, all facilities and installations are moved into the space created by the structural frame, creating a free plan for the museum inside but also articulating those elements within the area of the façade.

137. Sauerbruch Hutton, fire and police station, Berlin, 1999–2004. Façade of existing building and addition.
138. Sauerbruch Hutton, fire and police station, Berlin. Floor plan.
139. Sauerbruch Hutton, fire and police station, Berlin. Façade showing new volume overlaying historic base volume and wall.
140. Sauerbruch Hutton, offices for KfW banking group, Frankfurt, 2006–2010. Façade.
141. Sauerbruch Hutton, offices for KfW banking group, Frankfurt. Details of double layered façade.
142. Sauerbruch Hutton, offices for KfW banking group, Frankfurt. Airflow and ventilation section diagram.

The colorful gradations of the skins in the work of **Sauerbruch Hutton** have eliminated formal exuberance,[139] being less interested in a signature sculpture than in a smart and often playful system, which is consciously integrated into the urban context. In such a design, the skin is presented as an intelligent wrapper that has to be examined more closely to grasp its details and that offers a close link to Modernism with simple volumes and modular curtain walls. Sauerbruch and Hutton have succeeded in creating low-consumption buildings by harnessing the façades and their elements. According to architecture theorist Barry Bergdoll, »Over and over again the unloved legacy of discredited Modernism and urban renewal strata are found to be ›almost alright‹ by Sauerbruch Hutton, taken up in a new design that transcends them, re-contextualizes them, without condescension or nostalgia.«[140] The fire and police station in Berlin contrasts a new glazed volume with a glass façade ranging from a variety of reds to multiple greens with an existing structure. The low horizontal volume complements and contrasts the existing structure. The offices for the kfW Bankengruppe feature a layered façade providing ventilation space as well as a complex texture defining the character of the building. Many of Sauerbruch Hutton's buildings present as well-integrated precious packages that fit tightly into an urban or natural landscape. The patterns, colors, and materials suggest a glittering optic game until one approaches the buildings more closely and the intrinsic dynamicism of the parts becomes clear.

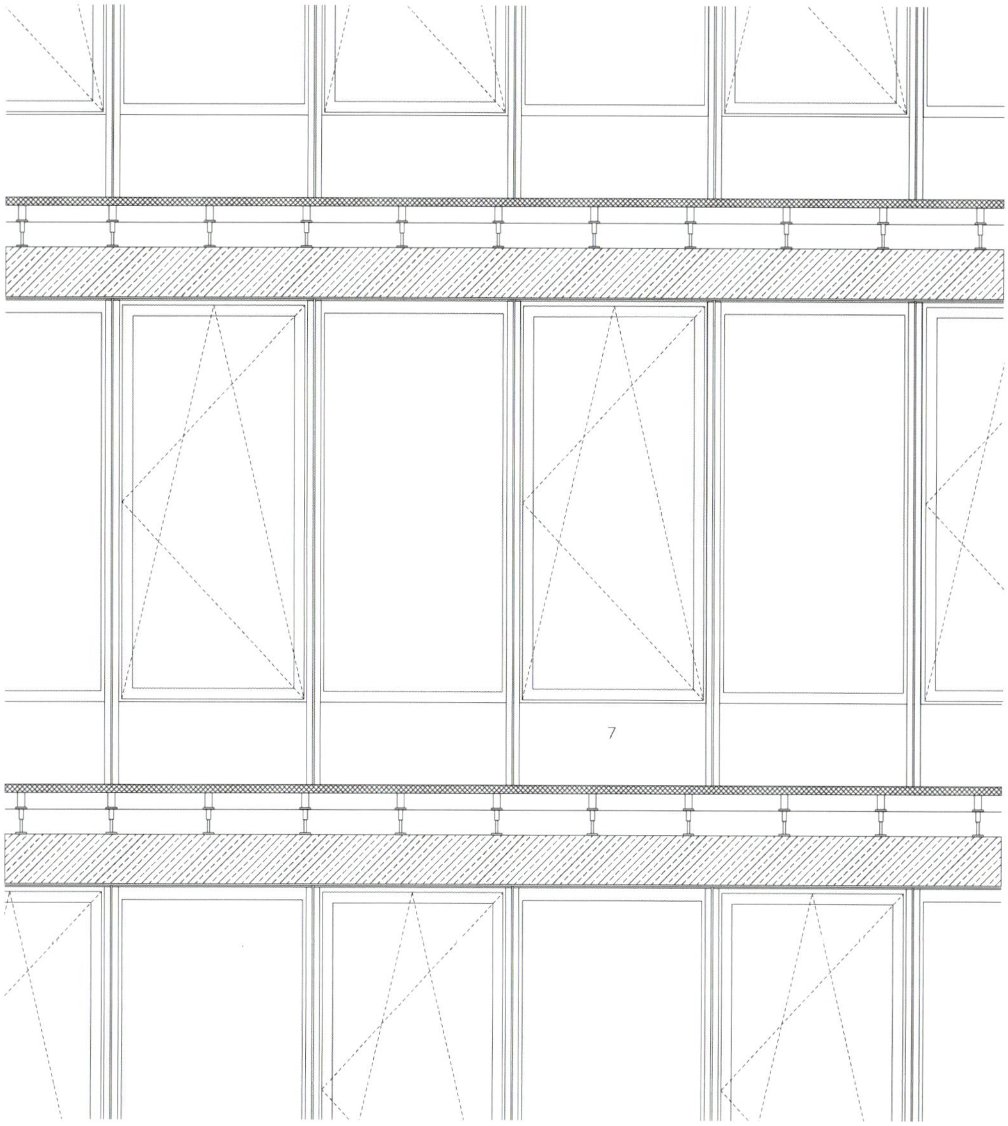
7

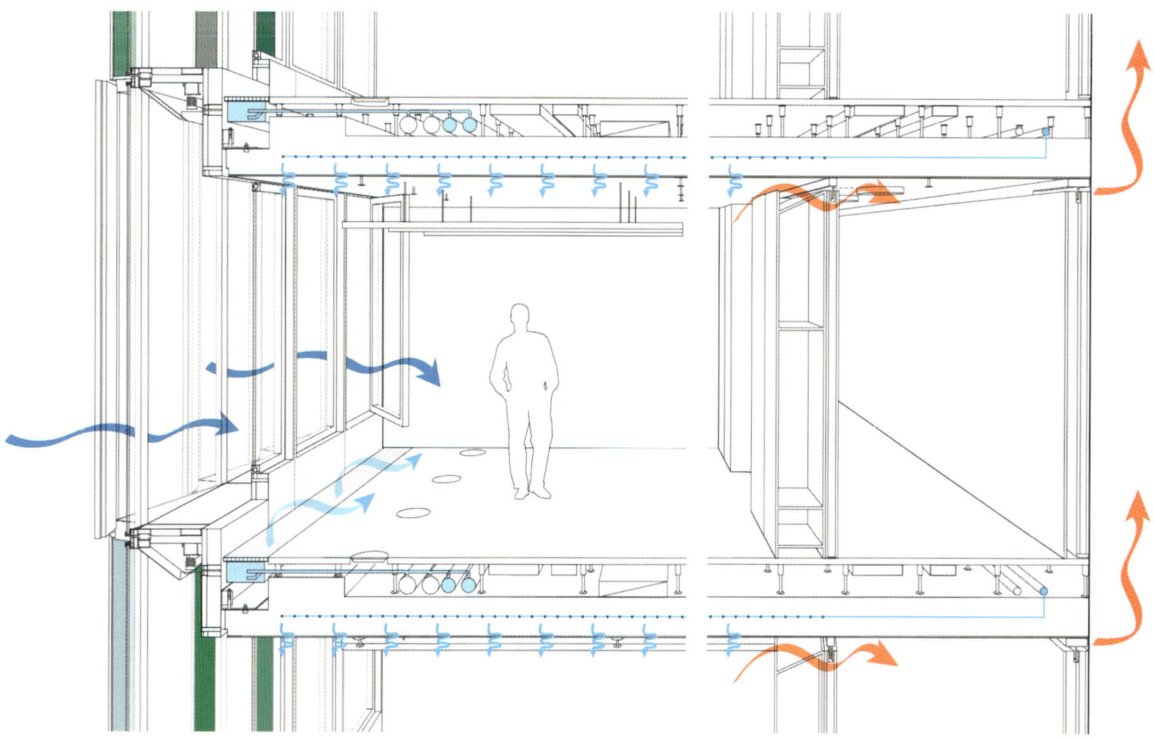

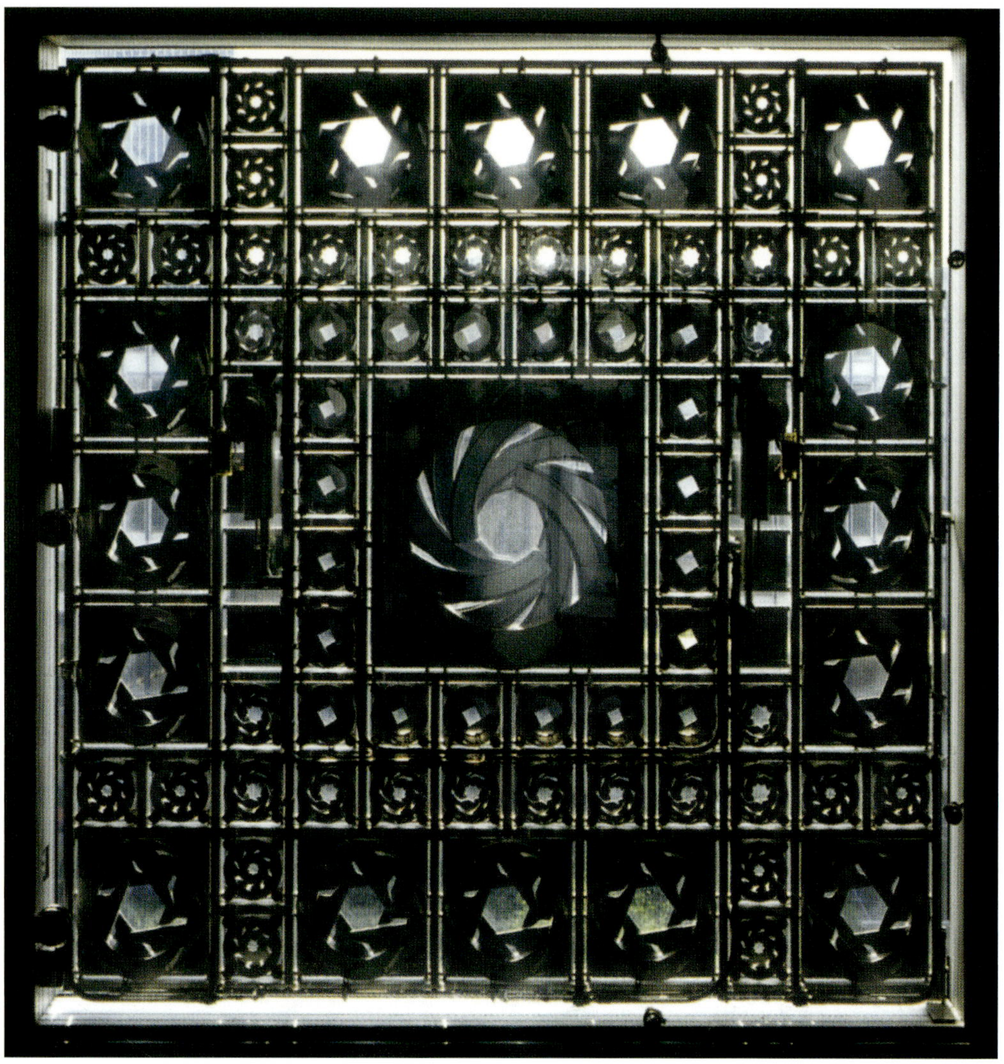

143. Jean Nouvel, Institut du Monde Arabe, Paris, 1981–87. Facade with dynamic sunshading elements.
144. Jean Nouvel, Institut du Monde Arabe, Paris. Detail of active façade elements that react to the intensity of the sun.
145. Jean Nouvel, Fondation Cartier, Paris, 1991 to 1994. Façade with glass skin running beyond building volume.

The French architect **Jean Nouvel** has used façades as a formal tool, while addressing sun shading, for example, as in the Institut du Monde Arabe in Paris (1981–87). In later projects, he further develops the notion of the multimedia façade, in which a building´s envelope provides a layer of information through motion and change. Nouvel's headquarters for the Cartier Foundation in Paris shows the diversification of glass screens as the outer skin of a building. In this project, the façade is visible as an independent structure, illustrating its separation from the building and its ability to interact with the surrounding park. The park is intended to enter the building and connect nature with structure: »The trees in the gardens and along the boulevard are reflected and refracted in the three inter-playing screens – they float in an abyss confusing the eye and defying reason.«[141] The glass screens define and simultaneously blur the transition between the interior and exterior, the building and the park. The façade's independent function is apparent as it extends beyond the building volume, becoming the expression of the building; the formally different shapes of the building's volume and the outer skin intensify the separation. As a result, the building seems to be composed of various vertical planes instead of defined volumes.

Thom Mayne and his firm Morphosis have long united urban issues and building solutions. His buildings feature independent skins and façades that function as sun-shading screens in appropriate orientations but simultaneously characterize the intellectual space that the buildings occupy. Instead of trusting glass for transparency, Mayne uses semi-transparent layers of metal to surround the buildings and create sculptural values based on folded and curved sheets rather than polygon volumes.

146, 147. Thom Mayne, 41 Cooper Square, Cooper Union, New York, 2009. Multi-layered façade: shroud for sunshading.

Conclusion

Layering as a physical and non-physical phenomenon is a broad topic that touches on multiple disciplines and ideas within the realm of architecture. This book reviews a theoretical history of primarily Western architecture as it turns to multi-stratified systems, but it also identifies what makes layering a conscious design tool and a basis of understanding spaces and their enclosures with an emphasis on architecture's cultural role.

As a system, layering ranges from a complex façade composed of many parallel parts (including color, light, and the communication of ideas) to a spatial configuration that one can move through and perceive simultaneously or that allows a phased organization of a building's program. Layering can be seen as a suitable tool for preserving an existing space while expanding its use and might be the only way to shift to a comprehensive sustainable art of building.

Layering is also an instrument to record time and continue the physical history of cities and buildings. Spatial layering acts as a vehicle to connect spaces that serve together in a transverse direction – in historic spaces as well as in contemporary designs. Material layering continues to be strongly related to façades and their energy performance, which requires building skins to be more insulated and to act dynamically and intelligently. In cases in which the formal repetition of layers is in the foreground, layering is a manufacturing method that allows many slices of minimally varying sizes to play a role in geometric deformation. Mass customization, CNC cutting tools directly linked to digital models, and the availability and use of composite materials encourage the application of material layering in contemporary design, leading to an a-tectonic type of design and construction that is glued and layered and that moves beyond the industrial model of mass production and montage.

The concept of depth is inherent in the multiplicity of elements in their different arrangements, depth suggesting intellectual and physical complexity displayed inthe buildings of today's society.

In interiors, color, material, and separate planes remain active to divide spaces into subspaces to accommodate exhibitions or for other purposes. Layering as a tool promises to transcend the boundaries of architecture beyond the individual building. Such an approach could call into question the division of landscape and volume, interior and exterior, and thus be a truly important element of the architecture of the 21st century.

Notes

[1] Rudolf Schwarz, *Von der Bebauung der Erde*, Heidelberg, 1949. Rudolf Schwarz (1897–1961) was involved in the reconstruction of Cologne, Germany, after World War II and wrote several seminal books related to architecture, specifically church architecture.
[2] Edward R. Tufte, *Envisioning Information,* Cheshire, Conn., 1990, p. 54.
[3] Ibid.
[4] Cesar Dante Maiorino, »The Effects of Composition and Layering on Secondary Grain Growth in Aluminum Alloy Thin Films«, thesis, Massachusetts Institute of Technology, Cambridge, Mass., Department of Material, Science and Engineering, 1986.
[5] Hans Leo Krämer, *Soziale Schichtung. Einführung in die moderne Theoriediskussion*, Frankfurt am Main, Berlin, and Munich, 1983.
[6] Willi Ule, *Grundriss der allgemeinen Erdkunde,* Stuttgart, 1931, p. 55.
[7] Wolfgang Viktor Ruttkowski, *Typen und Schichten: Zur Einteilung des Menschen und seiner Produkte*, Bern and Munich, 1978.
[8] William Lidwell, Kritina Holden, and Jill Butler, *Universal Principles of Design: 100 Ways to Enhance Usability, Influence Perception, Increase Appearance, Make Better Design Decisions and Tech through Design,* Beverly, Mass., 2003.
[9] Mary Carroll Nelson, »Layering: Approaching the ›Layer‹ as a Formal Element and a Significant Metaphor in Artmaking«, *Leonardo,* vol. 19, 1986, no. 3.
[10] Ibid.
[11] Ibid.
[12] Nancy Holt, *The Writings of Robert Smithson: Essays with Illustrations,* New York, 1979.
[13] Mark Linder, Lisa Gabrielle, Eugenie Tsai, Alexander Alberro, Suzaan Boettger, Cornelia Butler, Thomas Crow, Mark Linder, et al., *Robert Smithson*. Berkeley, University of California Press, 2004.
[14] Gordon Matta Clark, cited in: Stephen Walker, *Gordon Matta-Clark – Art, Architecture and the Attack on Modernism,* London and New York, 2009.
[15] Gordon Matta Clark cited in: Stephen Walker, *Gordon Matta-Clark – Art, Architecture and the Attack on Modernism*, London and New York, 2009. Gordon Matta-Clark made a similar remark to Donald Wall, although he focused more on the establishment of surface: » … what interests me more than the unexpected views that were being generated by removals is the element of stratification. Not the surface, but the thin edge, the severed surface which reveals the autobiographical process of its making – he is denying the modern form its existence, creating a fragmented unclear unrational structure, rendering absurd the principles of architectural form, revealing internal complexity.«
[16] http://www.nomart.co.jp/nakanishi/work_ex_2013_1.html.
[17] Leon van Schaik, *Spatial Intelligence – New Futures for Architecture*, Oxford, 2008.
[18] Vittorio Gregotti, *Architecture – Means and Ends,* Chicago and London, 2010. Gregotti continues, »This also often occurred in painting, at least until the mid-eighteenth century, in the great fresco cycles or in the established work habits of painters' workshops. Here technics seems to retreat before the complexity of the work, or, better, it tends to appear as crafts professionalism that determined its continuity in the name of the combined forces of innovation and the tradition of well-crafted work« (p. 61).
[19] Jürgen Joedicke, *Raum und Form in der Architektur. Space and Form in Architecture,* Stuttgart, 1985.
[20] Ibid.
[21] Dom H. Van Der Laan, *Architectonic Space – Fifteen Lessons on the Disposition of the Human Habitat,* Leiden, 1983.
[22] Ibid.
[23] Rodolfo Machado, Detlef Mertens, and Rodolphe El-Khoury, *Monolithic Architecture*, Munich and New York, 1995.
[24] Ibid.
[25] Ibid.
[26] Ibid.
[27] Ibid.
[28] Ibid.
[29] Donald Livingston Hanlon, *Compositions in Architecture*. Hoboken, New Jersey, Wiley Blackwell, 2009. Hanlon writes, »In contrast, spatial layering may be devoted to purely aesthetic purposes, as in Rome's Church of Santa Maria in Campitelli. Here the layers of space are entirely for visual effect, an illusion of deep atmosphere and ambiguous scale – an intense theatricality typical of Roman Catholic churches built during the Counter Reformation in Italy« (p. 79).
[30] Salvator-John A. Liotta, Kengo Kuma, and Matteo Belfiore (eds.), *Patterns and Layering: Japanese Spatial Culture, Nature and Architecture*, Berlin, 2012.
[31] Ibid., p. 61.
[32] Donald Livingston Hanlon, *Compositions in Architecture*, loc. cit., p. 79.
[33] Ibid.
[34] Cited in: Salvator-John A. Liotta, Kengo Kuma, and Matteo Belfiore (eds.), *Patterns and Layering: Japanese Spatial Culture, Nature and Architecture*, loc. cit.
[35] Fumihiko Maki, *Nurturing Dreams: Collected Essays on Architecture and the City*, Cambridge, Mass., and London, The MIT Press, 2012.
[36] Ibid., p. 153.
[37] Salvator-John A. Liotta, Kengo Kuma, and Matteo Belfiore (eds.), *Patterns and Layering: Japanese Spatial Culture, Nature and Architecture,* loc. cit., p. 53 f.
[38] Frank Lloyd Wright, *An Autobiography*, Petaluma, Calif., Pomegranate Publishers, 1943.
[39] James Wines, *De-Architecture,* New York, 1987.
[40] Leon van Schaik, *Spatial Intelligence – New Futures for Architecture*, loc. cit.
[41] Ibid.
[42] Zaha Hadid, keynote at ACSA (Association of Collegiate of Schools of Architecture) Annual Meeting, Miami, 2014.
[43] Eckehard Janofske, *Architektur-Räume: Idee und Gestalt bei Hans Scharoun,* Braunschweig and Wiesbaden, 1984, p. 48.
[44] Robert Venturi, *Complexity and Contradiction in Architecture*, New York, The Museum of Modern Art, 1977.
[45] Franco Fonatti, *Giuseppe Terragni: Poet des Razionalismo*, Vienna, Architektur- und Baufachverlag, 1987. Peter Eisenman analyzes the same building and talks about the decomposition of the elements with the building acting as architectural text in that the meaning of façades (also plans and sections) can be read as displacements. Peter Noever (ed.), *Peter Eisenman. Barefoot on white-hot walls*, Ostfildern-Ruit, Hatje Cantz, 2005.
[46] Thomas Herzog, Roland Krippner, and Werner Lang, *Façade Construction Manual*, Basel and Boston, 2004.
[47] Joseph A. Amato, *Surfaces – A History*, Oakland, Calif., The University of California Press, 2013, p. 18.
[48] Robert G. Ousterhout, *The Architecture of the Kariye Camii in Istanbul*, Washington, DC, 1987 (accessed through Google Books).
[49] Donald Livingston Hanlon, *Compositions in Architecture*, loc. cit.
[50] M. Hank Haeusler, *Media Façades – History, Technology, Content,* Ludwigsburg, av-edition, 2009.
[51] Robert Venturi, Denise Scott Brown, and Steven Izenour, *Learning from Las Vegas – The Forgotten Symbolism of Architectural Form*, Cambridge, Mass., The MIT Press, 1977.
[52] Ibid., p. 106.
[53] Pierre von Meiss, *Vom Objekt zum Raum zum Ort: Dimensionen der Architektur,* Berlin, Basel, and Boston, Birkhäuser, 1994, p. 116.
[54] Ibid.
[55] Alfred Breukelmann, »Die Wand, ein Medium?«, *Werk, Bauen+Wohnen*, 4, 1991, p. 26.
[56] Ibid.
[57] The engineer Brian Cody developed the concept that varying spatial conditions existed for the climate concept being used. Zone one consists of an unheated buffer between the first and second façade, in which elevators, service stairs, and traffic areas are located. Zone two consists of the individual offices, and zone three contains the open-plan offices, which are on the interior. Cf. Brian Cody, »Klimakonzept eines Verwaltungsgebäudes«, *AiT Spezial,* July 1996, p. 43.
[58] Jenny Lovell, *Building Envelopes – An Integrated Approach,* New York, 2010.
[59] Alfred Breukelmann, »Architektur der variablen Häute«, *Arch+*, 104, 1990, p. 54.
[60] Kiel Moe, *Thermally Active Surfaces in Architecture*, New York, Princeton Architectural Press, 2010, pp. 115, 116.
[61] Ulrich Knaack, Tillmann Klein, Marcel Bilow, and Thomas Auer, *Façades – Principles of Construction,* Basel, Boston, and Berlin, Birkhäuser, 2007. In 1981, working for Richard Rogers and Partner, Mike Davies had already formulated the idea of a polyvalent wall in his article titled »A Wall for All Seasons«. Here, several functional layers within a glass element were to provide sun and heat protection, and to regulate the function automatically according to current conditions. The wall itself was to create the necessary energy. The term »intelligent façade« derives from the concept of the polyvalent wall. Although the matter of technical realization has not yet been resolved, the polyvalent wall is the vision as well as the driving force for new façade technologies, and many scientists have been engaged in this topic over the last two decades.

62 Michael Wigginton and Jude Harris. *Intelligent Skins*, New York and Oxford, Routledge, 2013.
63 Jenny Lovell, *Building Envelopes – An Integrated Approach,* New York, 2010.
64 Vitruvius, *The Ten Books on Architecture,* New York, 1960, p. 52.
65 Ulrich Pfammatter, *Building the Future – Building Technology and Cultural History from the Industrial Revolution until Today*, Munich, Berlin, London, and New York, 2008, p. 157.
66 Ibid.
67 Ibid.
68 Ibid.
69 Amy Gardner, »Auguste Perret: Invention in Convention, Convention in Invention«, *Journal of Architectural Education*, vol. 50, no. 3 (Feb., 1997), pp. 140–155.
70 Ulrich Pfammatter, *Building the Future – Building Technology and Cultural History from the Industrial Revolution until Today*, loc. cit., p. 157.
71 Urich Conrads, *Programs and Manifestoes on 20th-Century Architecture,* Cambridge, Mass, 1975.
72 See also: Hanno-Walter Kruft, *Geschichte der Architekturtheorie*, Munich, 1985, p. 316.
73 Antoine Chrysostôme Quatremère de Quincy, *Jupiter Olympien: ou l'art de la sculpture antique considéré sous un nouveau point de vue; ouvrage qui comprend un essai sur le goût de la sculpture polychrome,* Paris, 1814.
74 Antoine Chrysostôme Quatremère de Quincy, *Dictionnaire Historique d'Architecture*, vol. II, Paris, 1932, p. 9.
75 Ibid., under the entry for »Façade«.
76 See also: Robin Middleton, »Hittorff's Polychrome Campaign«, in: *The Beaux-Arts and Nineteenth-Century French Architecture,* Cambridge, 1982. Middleton writes: »He thought to apply colour, inside and outside, to buildings. And in support of this programme he undertook detailed and thorough investigations into the use of colour in classical antiquity. For if it could be shown that the hallowed architecture of ancient Greece itself was coloured with paint, no other precedent for his present performance would be required, no further explanation needed« (p. 175).
77 Hanno-Walter Kruft, *Geschichte der Architekturtheorie,* loc. cit., p. 317.
78 Robin Middleton and David Watkin, *Klassizismus und Historismus,* Stuttgart, 1987, p. 284.
79 Hanno-Walter Kruft, *Geschichte der Architekturtheorie,* loc. cit., p. 327.
80 Ibid., p. 328.
81 Auguste Choisy, *Histoire d'architecture,* 1899, vol. I. Original text: »L'usage de recouvrir la pierre d'une enveloppe de poterie parait une tradition des temps où l'insuffisance de l'outillage rendait pénible la taille d'un parement régulier« (p. 285).
82 Ibid. Original text: »La peinture architecturale – ainsi que l'a prouvé Hittorff les monuments grecs étaient peints« (p. 295).
83 Robin Middleton and David Watkin, *Klassizismus und Historismus,* vol. 2, Stuttgart 1987, p. 228.
84 Hanno Walter Kruft, *Geschichte der Architekturtheorie,* loc. cit., p. 318.
85 Karl Hammer, *Jakob Ignaz Hittorff: Ein Pariser Baumeister,* Stuttgart, 1968, p. 125.
86 Franz Kugler, *Über die Polychromie der griechischen Architektur und Skulptur und ihre Grenzen,* Berlin, 1835, p. 38.
87 Ibid., p. 46.
88 Ibid., p. 10.
89 Karl Bötticher, *Die Tektonik der Hellenen,* vol. 1, Potsdam, 1852, p. XIV.
90 Ibid.
91 Ibid.
92 Ibid., p. 8.
93 Heinrich Hübsch, *Die Architektur und ihr Verhältnis zur heutigen Malerei und Skulptur,* Berlin, 1985; first edition: Tübingen, 1847, p. 33.
94 Ibid., p. 41.
95 Wolfgang Hermann, »In What Style Should We Build? The German Debate on Architectural Style«, in: Heinrich Hübsch, *In What Style Should We Build?*, Santa Monica, Getty Research Institute, 1992, p. 70.
96 Gottfried Semper, »Vorläufige Bemerkungen über bemalte Architektur und Plastik bei den Alten«, in: *Gottfried Semper: Kleine Schriften,* Mittenwald, 1979, p. 219.
97 Gottfried Semper, *Der Stil in den tektonischen Künsten,* vol. 1, Mittenwald, 1977, p. 228.
98 Gottfried Semper, »Vorläufige Bemerkungen über bemalte Architektur und Plastik bei den Alten«, loc. cit., p. 219.
99 Gottfried Semper, *Style in the Technical and Tectonic Arts, or Practical Aesthetics,* Los Angeles, 2004.
100 Ibid.
101 Gottfried Semper, »Vorläufige Bemerkungen über bemalte Architektur und Plastik bei den Alten«, loc. cit., p. 224.
102 Ibid.
103 Àkos Moravánszky, *Die Erneuerung der Baukunst: Wege zur Moderne in Mitteleuropa 1900 to 1940,* Salzburg and Vienna, 1988, p. 65.
104 Ibid., p. 46.
105 Gottfried Semper, *Der Stil in den tektonischen Künsten,* vol. 1, loc. cit., p. 228.
106 Hans Prinzhorn, *Gottfried Sempers Aesthetische Anschauungen*, diss., Stuttgart, 1909, p. 16.
107 Wilfried Wang, »In Search of Aura«, In: Rodolfo Machado and Rodolphe El-Khoury, *Monolithic Architecture,* Munich/New York, 1995.
108 Mirko Zardini, »Skin, Wall, Façade«, *Lotus*, vol. 82, 1994, p. 45.
109 See also: Pierre von Meiss, *Vom Objekt zum Raum zum Ort: Dimensionen der Architektur,* Berlin, Basel, and Boston, 1994, p. 199 ff.
110 Mark Wigley, *White Walls, Designer Dresses,* Cambridge, 1995, p. xviii.
111 Gerhard Auer, »The Desiring Glaze and the Ruses of the Veil«, *Daidalos*, vol. 33, Sept. 1989, p. 51.
112 Richard Weston, *100 Ideas that Changed Architecture*, London. 2011, p. 150.
113 Ibid.
114 Basel Kotob, *Spatial Layering: An Effect of Cubist Concepts on 20th Century Architecture*, master's thesis, Cambridge, Mass., MIT Press, May 1989.
115 Ibid.
116 William C. Seitz, *The Art of Assemblage,* New York, Museum of Modern Art, 1961, p. 10.
117 György Kepes, *Language of Vision: Painting, Photography, Advertising Design,* Chicago, 1964.
118 Ibid.
119 Ibid., p. 76.
120 Rudolf Arnheim, *Kunst und Sehen,* Berlin, 1965, p. 86.
121 Colin Rowe (with Robert Slutzky), »Transparency: Literal and Phenomenal«, in: *The Mathematics of the Ideal Villa and Other Essays,* Cambridge, 1976, p. 174: »We will presume the Palace of the League of Nations as having been built and an observer following the axial approach to its auditorium. Necessarily he is subjected to the polar attraction of its principal entrance which he sees framed within a screen of trees. But these trees, intersecting his vision, also introduce a lateral deflection of interest, so that he becomes successively aware, first, of a relation between the flanking office building and the foreground parterre, and second, of a relation between the crosswalk and the courtyard of the Secretariat. And once within the trees, beneath the low umbrella which they provide, yet a further tension is established: the space, which is inflected towards the General Assembly Building, is defined by, and reads as, a projection of the book stack and library. And finally, with the trees as a volume behind him, the observer at last finds himself standing on a low terrace, confronting the entrance quay but separated from it by a rift of space so complete that it is only by the propulsive power of the walk behind him that he can be enabled to cross it. Within this arc of vision no longer restricted, he is now offered the General Assembly Building in its full extent; but since a newly revealed lack of focus compels his eye to slide along this façade, it is again irresistibly drawn sideways – to the view of gardens and lake beyond. And should the observer turn around from this rift between him and his obvious goal, and should he look back at the trees which he has just abandoned, he will find that the lateral sliding of the space becomes only more determined, emphasized by the trees themselves and the cross alley leading into the slotted indenture alongside the bookstack. While further, if our observer is a man of moderate sophistication, and if the piercing of a volume or screen of trees by a road might have to suggest to him that the intrinsic function of this road is to penetrate similar volumes and screens, then, by inference, the terrace upon which he is standing becomes, not a prelude to the auditorium, as its axial relationship suggests, but a projection of the volumes and planes of the office building with which it is aligned. These stratifications, devices by means of which space becomes constructed, substantial, and articulate, are the essence of that phenomenal transparency which has been noticed as characteristic of the central post-Cubist tradition.«
122 Colin Rowe and Robert Slutzky, *Transparenz, Schriftenreihe der ETH,* Zürich, Basel, and Stuttgart, 1968, p. 27.
123 Ibid.
124 Ibid., p. 28.
125 Colin Rowe, »Transparency: Literal and Phenomenal«, in: Colin Rowe, *As I Was Saying. Recollections and Miscellaneous Essays,* vol. 1, Cambridge, Mass., The MIT Press, 1995.

126 John McKean, *Giancarlo de Carlo – Layered Places*, Stuttgart and London, Edition Axel Menges, 2004.
127 Anne-Catrin Schultz, *Carlo Scarpa – Layers,* Stuttgart and London, Edition Axel Menges, 2007.
128 Wolfgang Jean Stock, *Karljosef Schattner – Klaus Kinold. Korrespondenzen: Architektur und Fotografie. Correspondences: Architecture and Photography*, Basel, Berlin, and Boston, Birkhäuser, 2003.
129 Mark Wigley, »After-Life in Progress. EMBT 2000–2009, Enric Miralles Benedetta Tagliabue«, *El Croquis*, no. 144, , p. 23.
130 Ibid.
131 Raymond Ryan, *Work – McCullough Mulvin Architects*, Oysterhaven, Kinsale, County Cork, Gandon Editions, 2004.
132 Peter Eisenman, *The Formal Basis of Modern Architecture,* Baden, Lars Müller Publishers, 1963, p. 109.
133 Aaron Betsky, *Violated Perfection,* New York, 1990.
134 Peter Eisenman, *House of Cards*, New York, 1987.
135 Richard Weston, *100 Ideas That Changed Architecture*, London, 2011, p. 150.
136 Kahn, typed transcript of November 14, 1961, in a talk to the Board of Standards and Planning for the Living Theater, Board of Standards & Planning – N.Y. Chapter – ANTA, Box LIK 57, Kahn Collection. David B. Brownlee and David G. De Long, *Louis Kahn: In the Realm of Architecture*, New York, 1991.
137 Quantrill, Malcolm, *Juha Leiviskä and the Continuity of Finnish Modern Architecture,* New York, 2001.
138 Hitoshi Abe, Documentary, http://www.campuswu.at/en/event/d2-sc-event-abe/ (7/3/2014).
139 Barry Bergdoll, »Sustainable Colours and Non-Standard Forms. On Sauerbruch Hutton's Recent Work«, *2G*, no. 52, 2010, p. 4.
140 Ibid., p. 15.
141 Olivier Boissière, *Jean Nouvel*, Paris, Terrail, 1996, p. 138.

Bibliography

Addis, Bill. *3,000 Years of Design, Engineering and Construction*, London and New York, 2007.
Amato, Joseph A., *Surfaces: A History*, Oakland, Calif., University of California Press, 2013.
Arnheim, Rudolf, *Kunst und Sehen. Eine Psychologie des schöpferischen Auges*, Berlin and New York, 2000.
Bedard, Jean-François, *Cities of Artificial Excavation: The Work of Peter Eisenman 1978–1988*, New York, 1994.
Betsky, Aaron, *Violated Perfection*, New York, 1990.
Bloszies, Charles, and Hugh Hardy, *Old Buildings New Designs*, New York, 2013.
Boissière, Olivier, *Jean Nouvel*, Paris, 1997.
Bollack, Françoise, and Kenneth Frampton, *Old Buildings, New Forms*, New York, 2013.
Bötticher, Karl Gottlieb Wilhelm. *Die Tektonik der Hellenen*, Berlin, 1874.
Buchanan, Peter, and Dennis Dollen, *The Architecture of Enric Miralles & Carme Pinos*, New York, 1992.
Choisy, Auguste, *Histoire de l'architecture*, Paris, 1899.
Compagno, Andrea, *Intelligent Glass Facades: Materials, Practice, Design*, Basel, 2002.
Conrads, Ulrich, and Michael Bullock. *Programs and Manifestoes on 20th-Century Architecture*, Cambridge, Mass.,1975.
Eisenman, Peter, Rosalind Krauss, and Manfredo Tafuri, *Houses of Cards*, New York, 1987.
Eisenman, Peter, *The Formal Basis of Modern Architecture*, diss., 1963, Facsimile edition: Baden, 2006.
Fauchereau, Serge, *Braque*, New York, 1987.
Feireiss, L., and R. Klanten, *Build On: Converted Architecture and Transformed Buildings*, Berlin, 2009.
Flagge, Ingeborg, Verena Herzog-Loibl, and Anna Meseure, *Thomas Herzog: Architecture and Technology*, Munich and New York, 2002.
Fonatti, Franco, *Giuseppe Terragni: Poet des Razionalismo*, Vienna,1987.
Fortmeyer, Russell, and Charles Linn, *Kinetic Architecture: Designs for Active Envelopes*, Mulgrave, 2014.
Friedman, Donald, *Historical Building Construction: Design, Materials, and Technology*, New York, 2010.
Haeusler, M. Hank, Martin Tomitsch, Gernot Tscherteu, *Media Facades*, Ludwigsburg, 2013.
Hanlon, Donald Livingston, *Compositions in Architecture*, Hoboken, New Jersey, Wiley Blackwell, 2009.
Herzog, Thomas, Roland Krippner, and Werner Lang, *Facade Construction Manual*. Basel and Boston, 2004.
Hindrichs, Dirk U., *Facades: Building Envelopes for the 21st Century*, Basel and Boston, 2006.
Hindrichs, Dirk U., *Fassaden / Façades*, Basel and Boston, 2010.
Hittorff, Jacques Ignace [Ill]. *Jakob Ignaz Hittorff?: ein Architekt aus Köln im Paris des 19. Jahrhunderts* , Wallraf-Richartz-Museum, Köln, Graphische Sammlung, 21. Januar bis 22. März 1987.
Hobbs, Robert, *Robert Smithson: Sculpture*, Ithaca, New York, 1983.
Holt, Nancy. *The Writings of Robert Smithson: Essays with Illustrations*, New York, 1979.
Hübsch, Heinrich, *In What Style Should We Build? The German Debate on Architectural Style*, Santa Monica, Calif., and Chicago, Getty Research Institute, 1996.
Inoue, Mitsuo, *Space in Japanese Architecture*, New York, 1985.
Joedicke, Jürgen. *Raum und Form in der Architektur. Space and Form in Architecture*, Stuttgart, Krämer, 1985.
Kepes, György, *Language of Vision*, New York, 1995.
Klanten, R., and S. Ehmann, *The Sky's the Limit: Applying Radical Architecture*, Berlin, 2012.
Knaack, Ulrich. *Façades. Principles of Construction*, Basel, 2007.
Krämer, Hans L., *Soziale Schichtung: Einführung in die moderne Theoriediskussion*, Frankfurt am Main, 1994.
Kruft, Hanno-Walter, *History of Architectural Theory*. London and New York, 1996.
Kugler, Franz, *Ueber die Polychromie der griechischen Architektur and Sculptur und ihre Grenzen*, (reprint), 2012.
Laan, Hans van der, *Architectonic Space: Fifteen Lessons on the Disposition of the Human Habitat*, Leiden, 1983.
Lappin, Sarah A., *Full Irish New Architecture in Ireland*, New York, 2009.
Leatherbarrow, David, and Mohsen Mostafavi. *Surface Architecture*, Cambridge, Mass. and London, 2005.
Lidwell, William, Kristina Holden, and Jill Butler, *Universal Principles of Design: 125 Ways to Enhance Usability, Influence Perception, Increase Appeal, Make Better Design Decisions, and Teach through Design*, Rockport, 2010.
Liotta, Salvator-John A., Kengo Kuma, and Matteo Belfiore (eds.), *Patterns and Layering: Japanese Spatial Culture, Nature and Architecture*, Berlin, 2012.
Lovell, Jenny, *Building Envelopes*, New York, 2013.
Machado, Rodolfo, *Monolithic Architecture*, Munich and New York, 1995.
Maki, Fumihiko, Mark Mulligan, and Eduard F. Sekler, *Nurturing Dreams: Collected Essays on Architecture and the City*, Cambridge, Mass., and London, 2012.
Mark, Robert, *Architectural Technology up to the Scientific Revolution: The Art and Structure of Large-Scale Buildings*, Cambridge, Mass., and London, 1994.
McCullough Mulvin Architects, *Work – McCullough Mulvin Architects,* Oysterhaven, Kinsale, 2004.
McKean, John, *Giancarlo De Carlo: Layered Places*, Stuttgart and London, 2004.
Meiss, Pierre von, and K. Anding, *Vom Objekt zum Raum zum Ort: Dimensionen der Architektur*, Basel, 1994.
Meiss, Pierre von, *Elements of Architecture: From Form to Place*, London and New York, Routledge, 1990.
Middleton, Robin, and David Watkin, *Klassizismus und Historismus*, Stuttgart, 1991.
Moe, Kiel, *Thermally Active Surfaces in Architecture*, New York, 2010.

Moravánszky, Àkos, *Die Erneuerung der Baukunst: Wege zur Moderne in Mitteleuropa*, Salzburg and Vienna, 1988.
Morgan, Conway Lloyd, *Jean Nouvel: The Elements of Architecture*, New York, 1998.
Moure, Gloria, and Gordon Matta-Clark. *Gordon Matta-Clark: Works and Collected Writings*, Barcelona and New York, 2006.
Murray, Scott. *Contemporary Curtain Wall Architecture*, New York, 2009.
Noever, Peter (ed.), *Peter Eisenman. Barefoot on white-hot walls*. Ostfildern-Ruit, Hatje Cantz, 2005.
Ousterhout, Robert G., *The Architecture of the Kariye Camii in Istanbul*. Washington, D.C., 1988.
Pehnt, Wolfgang, *Karljosef Schattner, ein Architekt aus Eichstätt*. Stuttgart, 1988.
Pfammatter, Ulrich, *Building the Future: Building Technology and Cultural History from the Industrial Revolution Until Today*, Munich and New York, 2008.
Quantrill, Malcolm, *Juha Leiviskä and the Continuity of Finnish Modern Architecture*, New York, 2001.
Quatremère de Quincy, Antoine Chrysostôme, *Dictionnaire historique d'architecture: Comprenant dans son plan les notions historiques, de scriptives, archaeologiques, biographiques, théo riques, didactiques et pratiques de cet art*, tome 1, (reprint), Boston, 2011.
Quatremère de Quincy, Antoine Chrysostôme, *Histoire de la vie et des ouvrages des plus célèbres architectes du XIe siècle jusqu'à la fin du XVIIIe: Accompagnée de la vue du plus remarquable édifice de chacun d'eux,* tome 2, (reprint), Boston, 2001.
Rappaport, Nina, *Layered Urbanisms*, New Haven and New York, 2008.
Rowe, Colin, and Alexander Caragonne, *As I Was Saying*, vol. 1, Cambridge, Mass.,1995.
Rowe, Colin, and Fred Koetter, *Collage City*, Cambridge, Mass., The MIT Press, 1984.
Rowe, Colin, Robert Slutzky, Werner Oechslin, and Bernhard Hoesli, *Transparenz*, Basel and Boston, 1997.
Rowe, Colin, *The Mathematics of the Ideal Villa and Other Essays.* Cambridge, Mass., The MIT Press, 1982.
Ruttkowski, Wolfgang, *Typen und Schichten: Zur Einteilung des Menschen und seiner Produkte*, Hamburg, 2012.
Schaik, Leon van, *Spatial Intelligence: New Futures for Architecture*, Hoboken, New Jersey, Wiley Blackwell, 2008.
Schittich, Christian, *Glass Construction Manual*, Basel and Boston, 2007.
Schultz, Anne-Catrin, *Carlo Scarpa – Layers*, Stuttgart and London, Edition Axel Menges, 2007.
Schwarz, Rudolf, *Von der Bebauung der Erde*, Salzburg, 2006.
Schwarz, Rudolf, *The Church Incarnate: The Sacred Function of Christian Architecture*, Chicago 1958.
Seitz, William Chapin, *The Art of Assemblage*, New York, Museum of Modern Art, 1961.
Semper, Gottfried, *Style in the Technical and Tectonic Arts; Or, Practical Aesthetics*, Los Angeles, 2004.
Semper, Gottfried, *The Four Elements of Architecture and Other Writings*, Cambridge, Mass., and New York, 2011.
Semper, Gottfried, and Manfred Semper, *Kleine Schriften*, Ulan Press, 2012.
Stock, Wolfgang Jean, *Karljosef Schattner – Klaus Kinold. Korrespondenzen: Architektur und Fotografie. Correspondences: Architecture and Photography*, Basel, Berlin, and Boston, Birkhäuser, 2003.
Taylor, Jennifer, and James Conner, *The Architecture of Fumihiko Maki*, Basel and Boston, 1999.
Tsai, Eugenie (ed.), Alexander Alberro, Suzaan Boettger, Cornelia Butler, et al., *Robert Smithson*. Berkeley, University of California Press, 2004.
Tufte, Edward R., *Envisioning Information*, Cheshire, Connecticut, 1990.
Tufte, Edward R., *The Visual Display of Quantitative Information*, Cheshire, Connecticut, 2001.
Venturi, Robert, *Complexity and Contradiction in Architecture*, New York, 1966.
Walker, Stephen, Gordon Matta-Clark, *Art, Architecture and the Attack on Modernism*, London and New York, 2009.
Weston, Richard, *100 Ideas That Changed Architecture*, London, 2011.
Wigginton, Michael, and Jude Harris. *Intelligent Skins*, New York, 2013.
Witte, Ron, *Toyo Ito, Sendai Mediatheque*, Munich, New York and Cambridge, Mass., 2002.
Yu, Mayine L., *Skins, Envelopes, and Enclosures: Concepts for Designing Building Exteriors*, New York , 2013.
Zahner, Walter, *Bauherr Kirche. Der Architekt Karljosef Schattner*, Munich and Berlin, 2009.

Index

Illustration credits

Atelier Hitoshi Abe 125
Bianca Albertini and Sandro Bagnoli, *Scarpa – Museen und Ausstellungen*, Tübingen, 1992 90
Jan Bitter 140
Svenja Bockhop 129
Immo Boyken, Heinrich Heidersberger, Eberhard Troeger, *Egon Eiermann / Sep Ruf – German Pavilions, Brussels World Fair 1958*, Stuttgart, 2007, Opus 62), 132, 133
John Breda 10, 11, 12, 15, 16, 26, 33, 34, 36
Arno de la Chapelle 118
Robert Clocker 14, 37, 116, 117, 137, 139
Yumiko Chiba Associates 8
Andrea Compagno, *Intelligent Glass Facades – Materials, Practice, Design*, Basel, 2002 47
William Curtis, *Modern Architecture since 1900*, New York, 1996 52
Office dA (Monica Ponce de Leon, Nader Tehrani) 73
Klaus Daniels, *The Technology of Ecological Building,* Basel, Boston and Berlin, 1995 45
Peter Eisenman, *The Formal Basis of Modern Architecture*, Cambridge, 1963 (Facsimile, Baden 2006) 109, 110
Peter Eisenman, Rosalind Krauss and Manfredo Tafuri, *House of Cards,* New York, 1987 111
Ingeborg Flagge, Verena Herzog Loibl, and Anna Meseure, *Thomas Herzog: Architektur + Technologie*, Munich, London, and New York, 2002 46
Franco Fonatti, *Giuseppe Terragni – Poet des Razionalismo*, Vienna, 1987 31, 32
Serge Fauchereau, *Braque*, New York, 1987 64
Foster + Partners 134, 135, 136
David Franck 126, 127, 128
Manfred P. Gwinner, *Geologie der Alpen*, Stuttgart, 1978 4
Heinrich Heidersberger 131
Ibagli, http://en.wikipedia.org/wiki/File:OSU Wexner_Center.JPG1 112
Juha Leiviskae 119
Donald Livingston Hanlon, *Compositions in Architecture*, Hoboken, New Jersey, 2009 13, 20
John Horner 74
Robert Hobbs, *Robert Smithson – Sculpture*, Ithaca, 1983 5, 6, 7
Eckehard Janofske, *Architektur-Räume: Idee und Gestalt by Hans Scharoun*, Braunschweig and Wiesbaden, 1984 27, 28
Gyorgy Kepes, *Language of Vision*, Chicago, 1964 65
Mathieu Lehanneur 69
P. Lameiro, http://commons.wikimedia.org/wiki/File:Santiago Cidade da Cultura 01-04.JPG 113
P. Lameiro, http://commons.wikimedia.org/wiki/File:Santiago Cidade da Cultura 01-20.JPG 115
Salvator-John A. Liotta and Matteo Belfiore, *Patterns and Layering – Japanese Spatial Culture, Nature and Architecture*, Berlin, 2012 21, 22, 23, 24, 25
Orietta Lanzarini, *Carlo Scarpa – L'architetto e le arti*, Regione del Veneto, Venice 2003 91
MM (photographer), http://en.wikipedia.org/wiki/File:RomaTeatroMarcello01.JPG 79
Duccio Malagamba 98, 99, 100, 101, 123, 124
Robert Mark, *Architectural Technology up to the Scientific Revolution – The Art and Structure of Large Scale Buildings,* Cambridge, Mass, 1994 51
Corinne Diserens (ed.), *Gordon Matta-Clark*, London, and New York, 2006 9
John McKean 83, 84
Michael Minn, http://michaelminn.net/newyork/urban_renewal/downtown/cooper_union/2010-08-04_15-29-30.jpg 146
Kiel Moe, *Thermally Active Surfaces in Architecture*, New York 2010 50
Mccullough Mulvin Architects 103
Robin Middleton, »Perfezione e colore: La policromia nell'architettura francese del XVII e XIX secolo«, *Rassegna*, 23, 1985 53, 54
Enric Miralles, Benedetta Tagliabue, EMBT 97, 102
Conway Lloyd Morgan, Jean Nouvel: *The Elements of Architecture*, New York, 1998 143, 144, 145
John McKean, *Giancarlo de Carlo – Layered Places*, Stuttgart, 2004 83, 84
Takeshi Nishikawa and Akira Naito, *Katsura – ein Ort der Besinnung*, Stuttgart, 1978 18
Eberhard Oesterle, Lieb, Lutz, Heusler, *Double Skin Façades*, New York, and London, 2001 48, 49
Giovanni dall'Orto, http://upload.wikimedia.org/wikipedia/commons/4/41/SiracusaCathedral-pjt1.jpg 75
Archive of Guido Pietropoli 88
Pottercomuneo, http://commons.wikimedia.org/wiki/File:Basilica Palladiana, daytime,_2013.tif?uselang=it 78
Christian Richters 104, 105, 108
Felipe Ribon 70, 71, 72
Colin Rowe and Robert Slutzky, *Transparenz*, Basel and Stuttgart, 1968 66, 67, 68
Luis Miguel Bugallo Sánchez, http://commons.wikimedia.org/wiki/File:2011-08-17Cidade da Cultura._Santiago de Compostela-C03.jpg 114
sauerbruch hutton 138, 141, 142
Anne-Catrin Schultz 1, 17, 35, 38, 39, 40, 41, 42, 43, 44, 59, 60, 61, 62, 80, 81, 82, 85, 86, 87, 89, 92, 93, 94, 95, 96, 121, 122, 146
Frank Schulze, *Mies van der Rohe – A Critical Biography*, Chicago, 1985 130
Gottfried Semper, *Style – Style in the Technical and Tectonic Arts; or, Practical Aesthetics*. Translated by Harry Mallgrave and Michael Robinson. 1st ed. Getty Research Institute, Los Angeles, 2004 55, 56, 57, 58
Yoshida Tetsuro, *Das Japanische Wohnhaus*, Tübingen, 1969 19
The Museum of Modern Art, New York 130
Jussi Tiainen 120
Edward Tufte 2, 3
Carsten Peter Warncke, *De Stijl, 1917–1931*, Cologne, 1990 63
Berthold Werner, http://commons.wikimedia.org/wiki/Category:Duomo_(Syracuse)-Inside?uselang=it#mediaviewer/File:Syrakus_BW_2012-10-06 14-32-24.jpg 76
http://commons.wikimedia.org/wiki/Category:Duomo_(Syracuse)-Left_nave?uselang=it#mediaviewer/File:Syrakus_BW_2012-10-06_14-36-04.jpg 77
Henrietta Williams 107
Ron Witte, *Toyo Ito – Sendai Mediatheque*, Munich, London and New York, 2002 29, 30